More Than Everything

MY VOYAGE WITH THE GODS OF LOVE

Beatrix Ost

TURTLE POINT PRESS

BROOKLYN, NEW YORK

Hunters

I am a fox. I am a man.
I carry my claws. I carry my rifle.
I shimmer in the darkness. I walk in the woods.
I breathe blue silver sky. I stop the red-orange sunset.
        We are Hunters.

                              Viva Kuttner

For my grandchildren: Ronnie, Viva, Luna, Christoph, Stella, Julian, Ava, Liam, Sophie, and Anna

Requests for permission to make copies of any part of the work should be sent to:
Turtle Point Press
208 Java Street, 5th Floor
Brooklyn, NY 11222
www.turtlepointpress.com

Library of Congress Cataloging-in-Publication Data is available from the publisher upon request

Design by Phil Kovacevich
Printed in Canada

ISBN: 978-1-933527-90-1

Contents

PART THREE

Before We Begin

ONE MUST HANDLE ONE'S OWN HISTORY CAREFULLY. One must not wound the living, nor insult the dead. I am owner of my past, and, at the same time, its victim.

Memory's locations are often mirages. Snapshots, visions of people I know, peer through the tangle of memory that I hold firmly once again, until they willfully or inadvertently hop from my hand.

Threads free themselves, impossible to grasp firmly. Scent of lilac, the twilight moisture beneath the arc of the bridge, whispering voices, glances through cigarette smoke, skate blades sharp as swamp grass cutting into ice. A yellow border rings the beak of a bird child. The grinding beneath my feet on the pebble paths in the garden.

There are things, even banalities, that are uncommonly impressive, the building blocks of memory. One is constantly stalked by parables, by spiritual states, that melt together with tiny impressions. The strict voice of my father, Fritz, his office door ajar. White thread on a woolen skirt. Saliva in the corner of a mouth as it speaks.

I spent my childhood on an estate near Munich: Goldachhof. We were like a receiving camp for relatives and friends the war dealt our way. We had food. Some years after the war, as the country tried to recover, they left our secure niche, one by one, to build themselves a new life, to find lost family members, simply to go home.

I remember these partings.

Many partings. My heart had two halves. In one, knowledge of transience. In the other, awakening curiosity about new things—new loves. And I grasped very early on that everything always repeats itself, that only the exterior changes, replaced by something else.

Yes, replaced—and there is Ferdinand, my first husband, that handsome devil, the scraping noises he made during his ritual pipe cleaning, which gave him time to consider his next seductive chess move.

I close my eyes, draw the curtain before the present, and let in the robust past.

Part One

The innocence of love guarantees nothing—nothing at all.

The Sphere

"WHEN I WAS STILL INNOCENT," as the song says—that is, before one is swept away by the irresistible force called love and loses one's innocence, a possession that never struck one as a possession. When I was still innocent, at the threshold between child and woman, when my mother still protected me...The stone sphere that lay on my desk came from that time.

I push open a door, and the sphere rolls with the buzzing tone of memory across a bumpy stone floor into the middle of a room.

In the spring of '53, I drove with my parents to Italy. It was my first trip to another country. My mother, Adi, was driving her Blue Wonder, our first postwar car, a DKW, a blue-and-black-painted cabriolet with soft, luxurious leather seats she herself had worked over with saddle oil. She was passionate about driving, while my father, who never learned, sat next to her like a nervous hunting dog and combed the stretch we were racing along for every kind of obstacle, getting on Adi's nerves with his exclamations:

Adi, watch out! A truck coming from the right!

Adi, a stop sign!

Please—over there, the bicyclist! He doesn't see you!

Allow the woman with the pram to live! Please!

Oh, God, a pedestrian is crossing!

My mother drove on, composed and cheerfully chattering:

Yes, yes, I can see it! Why don't you try looking at that waterfall up there to the right? The green bit next to it, with the moist haze...

In the rear-view mirror, the attentive eyes of my mother, which sometimes twinkled back at me; in front of me, the head of my father, with its ring of gray hair; all around me, the hum of the motor, which carried us through valleys into the higher Alpine altitudes beyond, only to deposit us in the southern warmth of the Italian climate upon our grand descent. Awaiting us there, along with the lighthearted temperament of the inhabitants, were the famous culinary delicacies and the fizzy, very agreeable country wine—

Perhaps you'll even see palms, said my mother, and laughed, thrilled.

Since she had spent the winter months of her childhood in Venice, she was our tour guide. We were driving the country road; there was not yet an autobahn on this stretch. You could bet money on it: in every valley, a robber baron's castle perched at a high elevation, agonized by the weather of the centuries, its noble inhabitants no longer tyrannizing the local people. And then, near the Italian border, in shocking contrast to an ancient little town with a bulbous golden spire adorning the church—some quite different fortresses, these made of concrete, bunkers blocking off a valley, indestructible bastions brutally reminiscent of the last war.

During the trip, my mother chatted herself into ever-greater youthfulness. The hours slipped past, with stories about her father's experiment: buying our destination, Burg Persen, to create an idyll, in the Rousseauvian sense, *retour à la nature*. Adi's parents, nicknamed Pülli and Blüschen, Pullover and Blouse, surrounded themselves there with friends and kindred spirits. Pülli jauntily tossed out his landscape paintings, Blüschen gave herself over to the Muse. The period: 1900 to the First World War.

Much later on, as a grown woman, I was invited to tea with friends in a house near Garmisch-Partenkirchen. Snow lay in high drifts. A narrow path led through the corridor of sinister evergreens to a Bavarian country house. Frescoes adorned the walls on both sides of the entrance.

The cold was so icy that one could see one's breath in the vestibule. The sweet scent of freshly baked cookies streamed in from a nearby room. A sheep dog wagged its friendly way toward us. We hung up our coats and hats on antlers. Along the tiled floor of the entrance hall ran a colorful, homey patchwork carpet.

Come on in, close the door, cold as a witch's teat out there, called a voice.

On the bench embracing a green tile stove, at the seductively inviting coffee table, sat an old lady with fresh red cheeks. A trompe l'oeil.

Scarcely had I greeted her and looked around the room when I had to steady myself on the arm of a chair. My childhood sprang across to me like an echo. On the walls hung the same mountain views, nature studies, and landscapes as in the home where I had grown up: the superb paintings of my grandfather Max Rossbach. The wall at the lady's back was adorned with a large mountain view, the companion piece to the Watzmann that hung in our home. Laughing, she handed me a photo album.

That is your grandfather Pülli, he often visited us here. There, look, the child, that is Adi with her long braids. And I am standing among them. A few years younger than your mother.

In another photo Adi's brother Adalbert played tennis with Pülli. Ball and racquet were suspended in midair, à la Lartigue.

Blüschen leaning on the fence, a parasol in her gloved hand.

Adi, on skis, with her leggings wrapped high up her leg, a skirt over them, a pullover, fur cap, next to Adalbert in knickerbockers and tailored jacket, visored cap on his head.

Pülli with Blüschen on a bench beneath a locust tree, grapes entwined behind it, in sepia.

Yes, there you see the two of them. They always stopped by on the way to Burg Persen.

We hummed along in the Blue Wonder toward our goal, our grandparents' idyll. In the distance, hills in the tender green tone of grapes; further, beyond steep cliff formations, gray steel knives, with white northern blankets of snow. Snuggled amidst them, the ribbon of the road unwound before us as we whizzed higher and higher. Suddenly it narrowed: on the one side by a wall polished flat by water, on the other an abrupt chasm. Scarcely more than a few bushes and we would be hurtling downward. Above us laughed the azure sky, with lamb clouds dancing.

Quite unperturbed, Adi called out: We're almost there.

From the height where we had clambered, the little town of Pergine was sandwiched between variations of green; right nearby, on its cliff, squatted Burg Persen, its buildings jutting out like old teeth from the solemn-satiny black pine mouth. We were now winding our way along little streets and lanes, past gnarled vineyards between mint-green meadows strewn with confetti flowers.

Overjoyed that her Blue Wonder had made it, Adi parked in front of a rusted-out iron gate. She had recognized it right away. Wild rosebushes held the door firmly locked in place and let only one person slip through at a time.

Fritz remained sitting in the car, the top open. He let the seat fall back as far as it could, pulled his Borsalino over his face, and made himself comfortable.

Come back soon, I'm taking a nap, he said from beneath the hat.

Amid the animated spectacle of a completely forgotten slice of nature round about us, Adi and I wandered up the steep path leading to the fortress. The buzzing of insects; the silent, colorful jumble of every sort of butterfly.

A hare shot out of the undergrowth and hopped a ways off in front of us. Birds swirled out of the thicket shadows, into the hot brew of the midday sun. On both sides, unrestrained rosebushes, their tendrils holding hands across the path. The higher we struggled upward, the more the evergreens lit up; a thicket of needles, rickety with age, bent over by the winds, clawed at the cliffs. On a gnarled bough squatted several ravens, holding their heads askance, screeching questions into the hot air.

And then we had arrived. Lavender scent announced the blue of an ancient grove. Gravel crunched beneath our shoes. The climb through the shrill, sultry abandonment had left us hot. Steep stone steps that led to the vegetable garden. The remains of a gazebo. A clematis, seeking a hold, astray in the branches of a gnarled apple tree. The collapsed walls of a cistern. A frightened frog hurled himself into the golden mud puddle.

And right there, as answer to our exhaustion, Grandfather's dream. Lilac and jasmine hugged the crumbling walls to the right and left of the entrance.

Adi pressed against the heavy door, nailed with rusted iron trusses. The doorknocker was missing; only the ornamental imprint of a metal plate with a hole in the middle revealed its long-past use.

We both leaned against the obstinate wood. The cleft widened. The hinges sighed in their bearings. With the last shove, something came loose and rolled clattering into the room. We squeezed through the cleft. On the floor, a mountain of bird droppings; up above, glued to the wall, the artfully fortified nest of a swallow.

The midday sun steep above us dipped the cruciform-arched room in twilight. Only a hint of the outdoors broke through the paneless window openings cut deep in the wall. On one side, stone stairs led upward, and there, in a small uneven spot, lay a stone sphere: gray, round, intact, the only living thing in this robust decay.

In the cool musty air hung spiderwebs spanning the cake ribs of the ceiling, full of fly and butterfly cadavers.

Here, in the twilight, Pülli's vision is slumbering, my mother whispered.

And over there you can see what is left of the frescoes. A table with bread on it, a bottle of wine in the middle of a flowery meadow. And here at the window stood a long oak table. That's where we ate.

Her eyes lingered on the place where the table once stood.

Yes, look over there on the wall, she smiled.

A muscular arm, a white, rolled-up shirtsleeve, swinging an axe. One could no longer recognize the face—it had been gnawed away by moisture—only the legs and a bit of lederhosen, and, right next to it, a girl in a dirndl and apron sitting on a stone, her dark hair braided into a crown, two little kid goats frolicking around her.

That's me! laughed my mother. The one with the axe is Adalbert, my brother. Ah, my father, Pülli, had no idea how one gets things done, but he loved it when other people were competent. He gave directions.

Adi and I went slowly up the stairs and further, through the rooms that succeeded one another up here. We wandered through the dim, colorful tumult of decades-long decay. A grape tendril snaked through a smashed-in window, a thief's hand. A bat skeleton, finely gnawed clean, lay on the gray wooden floor, surrounded by rat shit. In the corners, leaves, feathers, bird droppings. A deep armchair with a few scraps of red velvet bled in the twilight. Fallen down next to it, a washstand of rusted iron.

One actually bathed in such a thing, said Adi, or else just out there in the fountain. The loo was a wooden hut with a heart in the door. There in the garden.

We looked out the window. Below us, marked off by fruit trees and an olive grove, we could still make out vegetable beds, framed by stones. From outside, the sharp shriek of the cicadas pressed in; above us, in the cornice of the roof, cooed doves.

Suddenly, loudly and quite clearly, the shuffling of heavy boots across gravel. The sounds of nature withdrew into the background, for now one heard the winded breathing of someone who must have been running.

Who is there?! Adi tried to bend out the window, but the wall was too thick, the window too distant. She could not look straight down, only into the garden and across to the wall of evergreens, the black watchmen. I clambered up onto the window bench. But I, too, could only see the bit of path we came in on.

Hello! Is someone there?

No answer.

Now we heard shoving, creaking, rumbling at the door. Then it was silent. We went quietly down the stairs. As we arrived at the last step, the shadow of a figure stretched across the floor. Next to it lay the stone sphere. We took one more step. There, in the doorway, against the white hot day outside, loomed the black silhouette of a man.

The man stared toward us. He looked like Rübezahl in the fairy tale. In his right hand he held a cudgel.

We have just been looking around, my mother called out to the terror. He just stared at us with his mouth open, not moving away. Stubble cast a sinister shadow on his coarse features. His lower jaw was thrust forward. I was terribly afraid. The cry of the cicadas outside fell upon us like a fever. Even Adi was not sure what to do. The black figure had forced its way into this primal idyll and throttled our hearts. I ducked, pressed up against Adi's back. Our hearts were pounding.

Mummy, I'm afraid.

There was only one way out, and it led past the monster in the doorway.

Adi took my hand, bent down, and lifted the stone sphere from the floor. Keep quite still, child. With the strength she always bore within herself, the way others carry a weapon, she cried:

Make way! Vai via! Vai! Vai!

And with the sphere in her raised hand she went toward the sinister figure in the doorway. A groaning sound crept up from his breast. With his cudgel he banged against the door.

Vai, vai! Adi shrieked again, with the voice of authority.

One could not read his expression. Only our own trepidation was familiar to us. Would Adi hurl the sphere?

We were now quite close to him, heard his panting. He ducked suddenly, like someone seized with fear, hissed something incomprehensible, *kraaach irgganchuk*, stepped back, out into the sun, onto the gravel, further back, until he felt the gnarled lavender bush behind him; there he remained standing, now quite helpless, merging into the undergrowth, becoming a grotesque element, *nature sauvage*.

We ran through the door, ran past him down the path, ran down between the thorny bushes that cut our legs. We did not look around us until we finally arrived, quite out of breath, at the rusty-red iron gate, which now stood wide open. I came to an exhausted halt and started to cry.

There, right there, waited our Blue Wonder, with Fritz. Fritz was beside himself, his features twisted, wrinkled, full of worry. He held firmly to the car, walking-stick and straw hat in hand, his hair disheveled.

My God, there you are! Do you know what happened!? A man stormed past me with a cudgel in his hand. Stop! Hold up, Signore! Stop! Wait! I shouted to him. I wanted to stop him. He had a look that could kill, but he didn't react, simply ran onward. Without even noticing me, the fellow rammed open the gate so he could fit through. Ran up the path and vanished.

My God, if something had happened to you!

Maybe he was deaf and dumb, said my mother, now calmer. Perhaps he is the silent watchman. She dried her face with her embroidered handkerchief, still holding the sphere, the weapon, in her hand.

My father collapsed into the car seat, covered his eyes with his hand, and sobbed.

I have never forgotten this episode. It was a symbol charged, indeed burdened, with life itself. Innocent at first, then pregnant with the unforeseen, with the capriciousness of fate, with the invasion of a threat into a seemingly idyllic moment. Just as the innocence of love guarantees nothing—nothing at all.

A Farewell

I WAS THIRTEEN YEARS OLD. My parents still lived on our estate in the country. I lived in the Max-Josef-Stift Boarding School in Munich. They had picked me up there. My mother was chauffeuring us in our Blue Wonder through the city of Munich and further out through the suburbs to the airport.

I sat in the back seat; next to me was Lexi, Father's dog. I felt happy to sneak out of the dorm for a few hours, and also happy to see my sister, Anita, again.

I had put on my favorite summer dress, blue background, strewn with blossoms. I wanted Anita to admire me in it, even though it was still cold, perhaps March. But that was precisely why she would notice the dress. Even at this time I still felt like her accomplice, for I had been carrying around her secret like the treasure it had not been for several years.

It was 1953, the airport under hasty reconstruction. Lonely perspectives, colorless de Chirico. Unadorned building sites surrounded a broad plaza. Further off, miniature people shoved lorries about, cranes combed the gloomy sky. We wound our way in between chain link fences, warning signs, and war rubble, and parked our car in regulation fashion, where the arrows indicated. Fritz took Adi's arm and propped himself up heavily on his walking stick. His feet laboriously tapped their way up the gray stairs to the entrance portal. Up above, a rusty tin sign said "Riem Airport." Through the departure lounge strode American soldiers; way up on a balcony, several people observing the plane traffic were silhouetted in the glass windows.

We walked past the rows of waiting-room benches, the flower stall, the newspaper-and-souvenir shop, and pressed on toward a rotating glass door. My father stood still and pondered it: glass panes dissected him into pieces that did not fit back together quite properly. He hesitated. But then my mother pushed one of the panels aside and hustled Fritz on through.

Before us stretched a large dining room. At some tables people were chowing down; all turned to stare at us. My parents went slowly, accompanied by shrill restaurant chatter, past chairs and tables, toward the little group. Lined up against the wall opposite, a tableau vivant: my sister, Anita; her children, Franzi and Christine; and her husband, Heinz, next to a tired lime tree in a red pot. I had taken Lexi, who was reluctant to go through the revolving door, in my arms. Now she was squirming to get down.

Hello, there you are, said my father.

Chairs squeaked as everyone got up.

My sister thrust herself forward. With both hands she pushed her children, ages two and three, toward our father, who had never seen them. But her spontaneity somehow got stuck, like air when you are scared, when my father clumsily maneuvered his legs about. She had not seen him for years. She did not know him handicapped like this. He seemed small now, too, a withered tree, crooked.

Heinz stood at attention next to his chair, bowed awkwardly, rather stiffly. Heinz had always played the part of the outsider in our family, though for me he had a smile and a shy wink. Our mother beamed. She opened her arms to Anita; beneath them hovered the children like little chicks. Anita kissed me, her body warm and round, the scent of her hair and skin familiar. I felt how glad she was to see me, how we really did belong to one another, although we were a decade apart in years and just as far apart in character.

Encouraged by our gestures of overture, she proceeded to embrace our father, Fritz, who, with one hand on his cane and the other seeking a hold on the table, scarcely held up under her vehemence.

Let's sit down, said Fritz.

My God, Papa, sobbed Anita. My father settled himself in, wiggling back and forth like a dog, and finally sat down on the hard chair.

Finally we all sat down, and my mother, always ready with the appropriate gesture, pulled out all sorts of packages.

You have to wear these in the hot sun, she said, and pulled a red felt safari hat over the head of each little grandchild. Franzi had her father's broad face and blond hair, sitting on her forehead like a sunny straw roof. Christine looked like I once did, the family found. This must have been why she was so familiar to me, so I took her little hand in mine.

Like a soundtrack to our weighty greeting ceremony, freighted with so many hopes, an airplane droned down onto the landing strip.

That will be our aircraft, said Heinz, like someone who always knew everything, and his eyes followed it until it sank down past the chestnut tree outside.

Heinz twisted round awkwardly, his chin practically resting on the tabletop, to observe the toy landing even more closely. Then, leaning toward my father, he asked politely: How are you doing?

It never gets better any more, only slowly worse, answered my father, and looked past us into the distance. They haven't found anything and aren't going to find anything to fix MS. Not in my lifetime. He took a deep breath.

Oh, Daddy, sighed my sister.

Now, for *in medias res*. Do you speak English already?

No, but I'm learning.

I am glad that my friend Veit can use you in Africa. That is a great opportunity. Great opportunity, he said to himself with a nod. Anita, for you, too. Out there you can raise your children right. I have recommended you highly, in spite of everything, he said quietly, as if he had to forgive himself the generous recommendation. Conflict hovered over the table, a somnambulistic ghost.

Yes, many thanks, thanks so much, said Heinz, bowing and clapping shut at his midriff like a Swiss army knife.

Our mother glanced with a cheerful smile from one person to another around the table. No matter what the atmosphere, she held firmly to the original intent of the reunion. My father looked as if he were practicing drown-proofing, a technique for keeping oneself alive in arctic waters. Survivors of the Titanic reported it: use as little air as possible. "The only motion is a slight lifting of the chin." My mother, by contrast, practiced what one might call "thick skin." In the presence of her pessimistic husband she was always in a good mood, which in turn failed to improve his temper.

We ordered weisswurst with sauerkraut. The new Africans in particular were to tank up on sausages and the delicious sauerkraut, since in their quite altered future they were not going to get them any time soon.

You're thoroughly capable, said my father.

It seemed that what Heinz really wanted was to spring up and stand at attention. He puffed up his chest and winked at my sister. She smiled.

We ate and drank beer and chomped and raised toasts, although beneath the grubby orb of light hovering above our table there hung family pressure. Two factions were firmly stuck in the imperative of their feelings. This family drama, so old, so tired. The parents were still cross with their capable son-in-law. They no longer altogether understood their own reasons, and yet these feelings lingered...disappointment, betrayal, weakness, and love.

Were they cross with him because Anita loved Heinz and not another? But which other? Not everyone could make a marriage as perfect as our brother Uli's—he had studied brewing and promptly married into a major brewery.

Still, ever since Uncle Veit had hired Heinz, people could sit together at table again. Yes, that much was true. But express one's feelings? About what? There was nothing one could clearly have named. A ghost hovered there, this inexplicable resentment of my parents', whose presence everyone felt. The atmosphere affected Heinz least of all, for he was the man he had always been. Only in this hour of parting could he really appreciate what for him had been the incomprehensible happiness of going off to Africa with Anita.

My sister gazed expectantly at our father. She waited for a warm word, a kindly glance, a loving gesture—something of her own to take with her into the future.

My father said: Africa. And the word stood there with us.

Fritz had been in the war, stationed in North Africa under Field Marshal Rommel. He was a lousy officer, preferring to shoot the breeze with carpet merchants in the twilight of the bazaars rather than take part in Hitler's war of conquest. My father and Rommel enjoyed a friendship that saved Fritz's life, for in 1943, in the midst of the war, Rommel sent him back to his estate in Germany "to nourish the Volk." The Field Marshal added, "There you will be of more use."

Africa remained Fritz's great passion. Always present was his friend Veit, who lived at the foot of Kilimanjaro, having emigrated in 1920—a step my father envied and admired him for.

He turned to Heinz.

Capable is what you are—as if Fritz were repeating his thoughts aloud. This concession was the easiest for him. A fact. He did not use the familiar pronoun with Heinz, never had. They always kept a polite distance. And now a fleeting smile glanced across Fritz's face, from the eyes to the goatee to the mouth, hovered for a brief moment on Anita across the table, moved over to Christine and Franzi, munching red sausages, their faces red with the reflection of their red berets. The little smile, a shadow of the past, was immediately noted by Adi. She rocked back and forth in her chair, holding the grandchildren by the hand, and sang happily:

Wiedele, wedele,	*Inside out, upside down,*
Hinter dem Städele	*Out behind the town*
Hält der Bettelman Hochzeit.	*It's the beggar's wedding day.*

I held Lexi still, using my foot to pin her leash under the table, since now she smelled the sausages and wanted to get up on the bench.

Yes, yes, Africa, said my father again. Africa was always with us, an aphrodisiac for the temperament, a bowl of punch brewed from the longing for missed opportunities. Africa was sandalwood oil, heat, fata morgana, pools of water, jacaranda-blue streets, pink flamingoes, snakes like tree trunks, screeching apes, the scent of vanilla, a fine tree. Colors, colors, colors. And the ineluctable danger of this wild continent, dictated by Nature herself.

A sudden flash of the upright lamp bathed the room in sepia. Aroma of coffee, sent to us by Uncle Veit. This hour belonged to my father.

The long, thin shadow cast by a spear flits along the wall in oxblood. Disappearing for a moment, it jumps into the rectangle of light at the window. A Maasai watchman squats amid the indigo of the tree-lined wall, and, if one looks long enough, one sees the white of his ornaments lighting up, the warthog teeth, shells, glass, and also the teeth in the mouth of the dog that pants next to him. The guard sits with his back to the house, so that he can rescue himself with a leap if two will-o'-the-wisps burst out at him from the jungle wall.

A leopard? I ask.

Not just that, there are many dangers. That's why Veit keeps the Maasai warriors as watchmen. Mostly they just sleep, full of bombe, nigger beer. He laughs.

Black-and-white photographs documented Father's Africa, which he lovingly cultivated, every detail unforgettable. His Africa, which he knew only from

the war. The opportunity, missed back then, wove the thread of a dream through his days. Now Anita was going to live the life he had wanted so very much for himself, Adi, my brother Uli, Anita, and me; she was going to live that life.

You will surely do a lot of riding out there, said my father, and Anita beamed.

Yes, that will be our great luxury, said Heinz. We shall see, he added, so as not to seem too happy. In reality both of them would have liked to throw their arms around the neck of this father, this father-in-law, full of happiness and gratitude. But many things stood in the way.

1953. Few people traveled by plane. It felt as if my sister and her family were the only ones flying off into a whole new life.

When the brief reunion and farewell ceremony were over and my sister, sobbing, pressing her children to her bosom, had vanished from our sight, with Heinz, to begin her new future, my father, while he was still staring at the door, said to me and Adi:

Go on up those steps and keep waving to them!

With his cane Fritz pointed to the rectangle of gray sky at the end of a staircase leading up to the visitors' balcony.

He wanted to be alone.

The Bird of Paradise Dress

OUR HOUSE WAS ANCIENT, as old as a citadel, 500 years old, with walls a meter thick. One of our forests surprised you with the quarry from which the buildings and stables had been built. On the way there, black evergreens pressed closely together, above blueberry carpets so soft that the rain seemed to hover above them. Primal wild boars took swamp baths in puddles. We children held hands until we came to the edge of the ravine. All varieties of moss grew on the steep walls. Generations of snakes and salamanders. Tree stumps, if one bumped into them, dissolved into dust. Jackdaws nested in stolen nests, crows lifted off from the thick underbrush with hysterical cries. Anthills, rust-red, revealed themselves among ferns, growing there in the eternal twilight since the dawn of time. The impudent laughter of a fox.

In the entrance hall of the house, the ceiling was domed, carried on columns. Small medieval doors with iron handles led on one side into several low-ceilinged rooms; as if the rural contractor had reconsidered, the rooms opposite were higher, the windows larger, broader.

In the cruciform-vault kitchen there stood, once a month, a gigantic wooden trough in which the dough for the month's bread fermented overnight. There I could lie on the broad windowsill—it was almost a meter across—as if on a throne, and follow all the doings on the farm.

As soon as my sister was finished with the convent boarding school and came home, finally free, away from the nuns, my parents thought about marrying her off. Not that anything was said.

My mother's gaze followed her lovingly and critically. My sister was rounded, wide-hipped, simply full-figured. Her skin was polished, the color of olive oil. I had hair, Anita had "The Hair": black, shiny as lacquer, great quantities of it, which she wore woven into a wide, heavy braid at her neck. Sometimes it fell down her back to her waist like a horse's mane. She looked very much like our mother: fine, slightly bent nose, large, heavy-lidded eyes, brows like swallows' wings. She was very beautiful, and one had the urge to touch her. Even an eight-year-old like myself could feel that. I also felt that what in my mother was agility and mobility, my sister wore as a weight; this species of Mediterranean melancholy, which suited her exterior, and, in this family, belonged only to her.

I observed my family from the lucky position of being the youngest. I knew how my mother cared for Anita. I, by contrast, was left in peace: that one, Beatrix, you can raise, said Fritz to Adi. That became a catchphrase.

I was an old child. Yes. I studied everything around me very carefully. I could do it at leisure, as I was mainly left to my own devices. With my braids woven into a crown around my head, with a steep critical cleft between my eyebrows, I caught wind of many grownup matters and formed my own opinions.

My mother took particular care of Anita's body. That was simpler. Her spiritual condition was more difficult to grasp and to decipher. Mother, Anita, and I drove into town for massages. The massage was supposed to give her impetus and somehow change her. But as soon as she sat upon her horse, anyone could see that she already had a healthy share of will and drive. Probably she just did not feel like doing anything other than riding.

My sister mounted her horse and had it under control like no one else. She had grown up with ponies. As soon as she outgrew one horse, my father would give her another, larger and more powerful. At present she rode an Arabian gray, Bella. They had a deep connection. Sometimes she came home from a ride with her face scratched up, though she seemed not to notice.

My God, child, did that creature take off with you? my mother called out in a concerned voice.

No, Anita gestured dismissively. She just hadn't ducked fast enough to avoid a branch. She so enjoyed riding through the forest, on the soft mossy floor, between the high evergreens. Then she gave Bella the spurs and scurried up a bank, a little heedless. One saw her in the twilight, storming toward the farm at a gallop. Bella with Anita, half-human, half-horse. They seemed to be more in the air than on the ground. One heard the stomping of the hooves, the snorting, the groaning of the saddle leather. She flew high, sank back down, tossed upward, pressed downward, relaxed, free and compelled; clumps of earth flew about, a bird fled from its meadow nest with a long cry. The heron hurled himself from his post into the water. Anita was at the gate. Beneath her saddle Bella had worked up a foam of sweat. Bella's nostrils were flaring. Both were relaxed, dissolved, and the melancholy was extinguished from Anita's face. Not a trace of it. Her body strong and lithe. She was happy.

But nobody was asking about happiness yet. The war, that monstrous war, had after all only been over for a few years. For happiness, something elemental would suffice—like "getting out alive," or "a roof over your head," or "a job." My mother's cares were not exactly definable, but they surely had to do with some sort of happiness that she wished for her daughter Anita.

Sometimes a young man rode into the courtyard to fetch my sister. She would straightway saddle up her Bella and ride off with him through the gate, into the lane, veering onto a path across a field, with her still waving; we, too, until suddenly both had vanished from our view.

That is the new veterinarian, said my mother with that certain look.

He is too lame, said my father.

She's got to get out of here, said my mother.

Fritz and Adi stood there, wrapped in their thoughts. Father, tall and slender, a garland of gray locks at his neck. Wrinkles of strictness, and others etched by laughter, crisscrossed his face. He wore leather knickerbockers, a Bavarian jacket, a green vest underneath.

He wore his sorrowful mien. Anita ought to make a good match, marry a rich man. The opposite of what they had done. Their love had maneuvered them through thick and thin. The thread from which they wanted to weave Anita's happiness was drawn from the cloth of their love. That, too, they had forgotten, as if there were a new definition of happiness, as if love had been abolished.

Amid our frequent round of guests, my father was proud of my sister. He trusted she would make a coolly considered marriage. He had wanted that for himself, just as he did for Anita. After what we had all been through, money and success were more important. One could not yet properly imagine romanticism. It gave my father a certain pride that people wanted so much to touch my sister; she carried the dowry of Nature with her like a birthright.

The catch was that only a horse-lover could get along with her, since she had no other passions. This immovability made my father impatient—in fact, irritable. To lighten the atmosphere, people would make jokes about it. One of these jests became a household pun: "If only you'd married Schecker Pauli..." The imaginary Schecker Pauli has lots of money, but the girl does not want him, so she has to go through lots of unpleasantness. And again and again, when someone was hard up, it came as if shot from a pistol: "If only you'd married Schecker Pauli..."

The nineteenth century ended in Germany in 1945. In bourgeois families like ours the rebuilding brought new circumstances, new social structures. This was approached with great skepticism and adopted only hesitantly. My parents were appalled by what the war had brought about. Where were their friends' sons, the sons of the neighbors in their set? The war had torn a huge hole in the age group eligible as potential suitors for Anita. All that chaos. Amid the industriousness of the rebuilding, one again and again ran up against the sordid disorder and bestial plunder the war had caused in every part of our lives.

Another young man, Axel von Bohnin, a distant relative of Aunt Esther, dwelt in her run-down moated castle, together with her twenty Schnauzers. American officers inhabited one wing, which still somehow held up, while the rest of the medieval building, which seemed to be sinking toward the water lilies and into the moats, greeted us with a deeper bow upon every visit to Aunt Esther. The overgrown stone walls enwrapped the castle like a tired snake.

We heard the humming of a motor even from a long way off; it was still a great rarity. An American vehicle driven by a friendly officer brought Axel von Bohnin to our place to have tea while the officer was passing the time fishing in Father's waters.

Naturally my parents thought Axel came because of Anita. My mother sat at the table in the den. The tablecloth, at which she sewed in golden cross-stitches, fell like a second skirt across her lap, her feet, onto the floor. My father stood at the window, a cigar between his index and middle fingers, and observed Axel sauntering up to the house. He had supposedly been unfit for service. In what way unfit? That they could not quite ascertain. Although my father condemned the war and called Hitler the most fearsome catastrophe that had ever befallen Germany, there was something deeply military in his own manner, in his upbringing. "Unfit for service" was a stigma, somehow.

Maybe he's got something in him after all, my father observed.

My mother glanced up from her embroidery hoop.

He is from a good family.

The dogs barked. Axel walked beneath the trophy antlers into the room. With him, Kafka's "spark of a possibility." As my sister, who had been sought everywhere with whistles and loud calls, finally stood in the doorway, the antlers above her, this spark was extinguished.

Axel had joined my mother on the bench, taken the needle out of her hand, and started embroidering away with the greatest relish, golden cross-stitch after golden cross-stitch.

Which came first? My sister became an expert in dealing with parental expectations.

•

To rouse the sleepy band of lads who worked on our farm, my father had hired a young former officer as manager.

Heinz Seifert came from Saxony; it came through right away in his accent.

Military career? asked my father.

Ja, cavl'ry.

Do you have any clue about agriculture? my father wanted to know.

No, only horses. But I learn very fast. My mother sewed gloves, my father is dead. I worked my way up from zero, the military was my big break.

Astonished by this openness, attracted by the direct gaze, convinced by his attitude—"one can learn anything"—my father hired him.

Jawoll, said Heinz Seifert, and clicked his boot heels together. He was more stout than tall, with wide shoulders, an open Slavic face. He came across as bigger than he was, owing to his upright, rather stiff posture. Like someone who is concealing something but wants to give you the impression of having said everything, he looked with his clear blue gaze directly at his interlocutor, eye to eye. Very soon he had convinced my father of his competence.

My father stepped forth from the gate and tenderly gazed across his land. He saw Heinz out there on his horse, giving the lads instructions. Or was that him on the haymaker, bobbing up and down in the flickering afternoon heat? My father walked part of the way, propped on his cane, toward the scent of the fields, behind him the smoke flag of his cigar. His feet gestured enigmatically. At times they ran like thoughts, with no control, sideways; sometimes they did not want to move at all, which made his step appear delayed.

Fritz had had everything under control. The people who worked for him, the potato cultivation, the team of horses—often one believed he controlled even the weather. When he looked up to the sky to map out the next 24 hours with the aid of a cloud formation: always correct.

Now he looked upward, but the sky seemed to disappoint him. The seed-beds that grew in rows over by the creek were too far away. Someone had to be sent down there to bring him a report.

Fritz stood on the packed dirt of the road, alone, isolated from the life-energy of the others. Old he still was not. A woodpecker loudly pecked Fritz's anxiety into the bark, quite nearby. Tack tack tack tack tack. Would they find him if he hurtled down the steep embankment at the side of the road? he wondered. His dog jumped high up on him in greeting and he seemed frightened half to death.

Over there, across the field, by the heads of cabbage, he saw the rider, Heinz, changing from a trot into a gallop.

It seems to Fritz that he himself is on his steed. He hears behind him the rushing, roaring and pressing of eighty stallions, driven from their stalls, fleeing the insane fire and smoke, following him. He feels their breath, hears the anxious clip-clop of their hooves, the cries of the lads that hold the horses together. He rides on ahead, behind him a red wall of fire. And yet he himself is calm. Duty gives him strength. He does not feel the hard ground; it seems to him as if he is hovering along the brook toward the rescuing meadow, a little further; behind him rush the snorting creatures; already he reaches the pasture fence post, the big pasture, the opening. He rides through and sweeps out a broad arc in the corral, brings them all to safety.

Lost in thought, he wandered some distance down the gravel road, then, as if he had forgotten something, came to an abrupt stop, looked once more far out across the flat country, squinted, puffed on his cigar, turned and went off, slowly, with short, careful steps, back toward the farm buildings. He felt unusually tired. As for the man who had set out a short while earlier—he scarcely still resembled him. Those were the signs.

The mysterious illness that had seized control of his legs was later diagnosed as multiple sclerosis. No one talked about "the illness." Fritz forbade it. He hated being ill. He was not ill.

Him I can rely on. Immensely diligent fellow, said my father, meaning Heinz, out there in the field. That he could ride so well also pleased him.

Reliable fellow.

My mother nodded, happy that her Fritz had someone at his side.

And so it came about that Heinz often sat with us at table.

•

My sister wove a red ribbon through her braid.

The bird of paradise dress. I would never forget this dress of my sister's. Was it the yellow of sunflowers, or a yellow that lights up from autumn leaves, or in the evening sky? No, it was saffron, deep yellow, as one knows it only in exotic plants. On the saffron background of the silk, blue and emerald-green birds of paradise with feathered trains capered about beneath palms. In one's hand the silk had an exotic tenderness. My mother had got hold of a piece of this fabric in exchange for comestibles. Even many years after the war, barter helped circulate the most wondrous goods.

First came the red ribbon in her hair, then my sister wanted pumps. She skipped down the stairs on tiptoe to practice.

When, please? she asked impatiently.

Buying shoes meant a trip into the city.

With the urgency and attentiveness that Anita otherwise mustered only during the purchase of a saddle or bridle, the tailor was scheduled into the house to sculpt the exotic fabric. The dress was built like couture around Anita's body; when the stitching was finished, it hugged her figure, the sleeves ruffled at the elbow, plissé pleats resting densely on her breast, down to her waist, the skirt reaching almost to the ankles. Standing on her new pumps, Anita looked insanely beautiful.

I knotted Father's necktie about my thin waist, above a dress my mother had brought from Bulgaria. It too was silk, ruffled at the shoulders, embroidered with little cross-stitches. I found myself beautiful too.

In his free hours Heinz Seifert sat at the edge of our garden, under the weeping willow, or at the corral, leaning on a post with a book in his hand. One hour every day for continuing education.

Anita and I joined him.

Are we disturbing you?

He told us about the war. Male episodes. About insoluble situations he had solved. We nodded. He told of the rain that the sun gathers back in again. Of the logical sequence of events in nature.

The rainbow is the bridge of the gods, he said.

Beautiful, said Anita, and smiled.

He read us a poem he had just written for her.

Read it again, said my sister, her face red, and gazed out past him, at some place far away, in the dark ribbon of woods. Anita looked at her hands, which rested. one atop the other, on the fence post, brown and soft, muse's hands, with no veins, with finely tapered fingertips. She looked down to the molehill a mole had freshly heaped up just a little while earlier, before we had met at the fence. She looked at her feet in the open sandals, soft, round, and brown, siblings of her hands.

What had he said?

I lingered close by, neither invited nor sent away. I felt the weight of this meeting.

Are you one from the meadow, one from the garden
In the bunch of flowers in my hand?

he had asked in the second verse. Anita smiled. His deep voice sounded strange and new to her, like something neither of us had yet heard, like the purring of a motor in the concert round about us, yes, like the automobiles that now and then interrupted the music of rural life. From quite far away, behind the fields, behind the forest, we heard the cuckoo cry "cuckoo, cuckoo".

Heinz stood before Anita, not tall, only a little taller than she, his wide Slavic head leaning to one side. Earnest. When he read, and then looked up from the page, his eyes swept her in, like a butterfly net. The bumblebee that buzzed around him, the scarab beetle that struggled its way up his collar, melted in with the panting dog in the grass. Heinz's presence possessed a vehemence that Anita could not explain. Drops of sweat gathered on his brow. He fumbled for his handkerchief and Anita was frightened. The butterfly net lifted itself, the loud meadow sang and chirped, it buzzed, the dog panted.

Anita! Anita! came the voice of my mother floating over to us. I went running off.

Are you one from the meadow, one from the garden came the afterbuzz.

Anitaaa! Can you fetch parsley?

Yes, she called, cried: Yess!

A glance back. Heinz had disappeared. The fence enclosed the meadow; the shadow of the trees lay, blue, between house and pond.

·

With Heinz among us we had a coachman again. It was superb to sit between Anita and Heinz up front in the wagon. The soft body of my sister on the one side, on the other Heinz's taut muscles, the strength of his energy. Now many things were easier. One no longer had to force Anita to go for a massage. In the village, in front of a shed behind Mrs. Hagenreiner's colonial goods store, we tied up the horses and waited for my sister. Heinz and I sat on a little wall next to the rabbit hutch. The rabbits jostled at the wire door, pressed their noses through the spaces between the wire meshes, to nibble at the blades of grass I pushed through to them. There was grass in the courtyard between the wagon tracks. I looked vainly for lions' tooth. That is what they would have liked most. But then I slipped back closer to Heinz, to listen to him. He explained to me how the horse holds energy in its breast to pull the wagon. How the legs elegantly play into the musculature at a canter and at a gallop. How the carriage is a clever invention, merging with the horse into a greater whole.

Although I was the only one in the family not interested in horses—on the contrary, I was afraid of them—it was quite splendid to know Heinz's attention was fully concentrated on me. This present made me a trusted ally. When on a carriage ride, I sat in the middle and felt at my back how Anita and Heinz held hands. Then I got to hold the reins. I bent forward and observed with playful attention the muscles on the hindquarters of Janosh and Bella, to please Heinz.

As soon as we reemerged with our coach from the loyal shadow of the forest, saw our farm further off as a chess piece standing on the orderly board of the fields, Heinz and Anita fell away from one another, like the pages of an opened book. Heinz took the reins once again, and I leaned back again into the mysterious middle.

My father liked to chat. He liked it best when as many people as possible listened to him. In order not to have to admit his weakness, Fritz called it talking shop. And this was why Heinz had come to sit with us at table. The other farm hands ate in the big dining room near the kitchen. There, there was loud smacking of lips. Dipping of bread in milk. Belching. Loud slurping of soup. Everything that was forbidden us at table. Heinz sat opposite me, as guilty as any of them.

My mother's gaze did the rounds critically. Beatrix! Fork to mouth, not vice-versa! No shoveling it in! she said unambiguously. Heinz felt this addressed to him, too.

Well, how is it? he asked me, to unburden himself of his embarrassment. He propped the elbow of the hand that guided the spoon to his mouth on the table and bent down to his plate. His hand trembled a little. He avoided looking at Anita and concentrated on my father's utterances, which amidst the dining ceremony changed subjects with unexpected quickness, shooting out like blank cartridges.

It was a game: Heinz against my impatient father. Heinz stimulated my father above all because he gave him his entire attention. And Father liked to eat and make conversation, in both cases with great relish.

Heinz came from Saxony, from a village near Chemnitz—my mother's family also came from Saxony. My father liked to tell the story of my Saxon great-grandfather, Arved Rossbach, a tall, dignified, very good-looking man who had built many significant buildings in Leipzig and Dresden at the end of the nineteenth century: the opera house, the railway station, the chancellery, banks and villas. My mother had gone visiting there as a young girl.

All of it destroyed by the Russians in the war, said my father. Now they have changed their mind and are proud of Arved, because of his communitarian convictions. He built the first workers' housing estate with running water and toilets. 1900—think of it.

The conversation leaped like a ball from my grandfather to Old King Fritz to the Meissen porcelain we ate on every day—my mother had inherited a banquet setting for 24 people. Then it veered off onto the Saxon landscape. This Heinz knew very well. He nodded in agreement.

Flat, the land is very flat, said my mother, and looked out the window to picture it to herself. The flatland. All the way through to the chalk cliffs on the island of Rügen, which once belonged largely to my family, to Arved Rossbach's forebears.

Yes, they were very wealthy, said my mother. She drew herself up in her chair and had to smile.

Heinz perhaps reflected that he had forebears, too, but no one cared a fig about them. Least of all he himself. Not worth mentioning. And, as if my father had read Heinz's thoughts, he bent down to him in a friendly way, with genuine interest.

Didn't you say your mother sewed gloves for a living? Hmm, that's a tough row to hoe.

Yes, we were very poor, said Heinz with a laugh. He laughed, because he was thinking about what he was going to say next. Poor? Back then, when I was growing up, we were poor. Not any more. Each week I send my mother in East Germany a care package with coffee, wool, aspirin, and silk stockings, and she can barter things for them. By their standards she is not poor any more. There is not a lot to buy among the Russians, but one can barter for help and many other things. A real black market is in bloom out there.

He laughed even more, this time about his luck at being here in Bavaria. As he did so he twinkled at me. My sister was silent. She petted a dog that was begging, under the table, on her side. Her whole attention concentrated itself on Father. She chewed slowly, looked around the table, petted the dog again, and when the conversation turned to horses, then and only then did she join in, always addressing Father, since it pleased him.

Apropos the Russians, my father said. Max Rossbach, Arved's oldest son, my wife's father, who of course grew up in Dresden…Anyway, Max went to the Russian school in Dresden. At the time that was very unusual. He spoke fluent Russian.

Heinz nodded. He was already in the picture when it came to family history.

Yes, my father continued. In the 1914 war, Max received a special captain's commission because of his language skills. He was to turn up at the German-Swiss border. There he received his orders with his platoon, about twenty men, to take over a sealed train and accompany it all the way across Germany. At every stop his platoon had to swarm out in formation, to secure the train under the heightened conditions.

My father took off his glasses, raised his eyebrows and looked across the table to his wife, who embodied that cross-section of humanity that has no clue about the rules of war. Heinz had long since given a nod of agreement.

"Heightened conditions" means firing your weapon immediately, should the sealed car open, for instance, or someone approach. In Sassnitz, on the island of Rügen, the train was handed over to Swedish military personnel. So. Max found out only much later who was in the train. It was Lenin, who, in the event of an escape, was to be addressed in Russian and arrested. Lenin, who had emigrated to Switzerland in 1901, was now being shipped back to Russia with German help. Once he arrived there, he toppled the Kerensky regime—naturally it had all been prepared in advance—triggered the October Revolution, and became head commissar of the Supreme Soviet and founder of the Soviet Union.

That's all gone down in history, said Heinz. Unthinkable that Lenin might have gotten loose in Germany.

I see you are no Communist, said my father contentedly.

He went to the bookshelf, looked along the rows, pulled out a book—Broaden your horizons, young man!—and pressed Nietzsche into Heinz's hand.

Heinz was a superb listener, Father a superb storyteller. Thus they formed a sort of alliance, a mutual dependency, a symbiosis. What one wanted to unload, the other eagerly sucked in. A good listener seduces the narrator. The seduction is as intimate, quiet, unannounced as love itself. The listener makes the narrator reveal a great deal of himself—perhaps everything. The narrator goes into a wonderful intoxication that leaves him blind. Deaf too.

Thus Heinz became our family's familiar.

My Sister Becomes a Beast

DURING THIS PERIOD, there in our house, Anita and I shared a room. Upstairs on the second floor, a wide corridor separated ours from our parents' bedroom.

Anita's bed stood at the window, mine against the wall in the opposite corner of the big rectangular space. Between them stood a cupboard with two flying doors and sides of glass, so that one could see through. In its interior dwelt Anita's glass menagerie. Tiny fillies stood on glass legs, played with glass mares on glass grass. Piglets suckled at the glass teats of their glass mother sow. Green parrots, birds of the most various kinds, perched on glass boughs. Chickens consorted with a rooster. Kittens slept or played with marbled spheres, a white glass steed reared up, the icy leaves of trees overshadowed a group of sheep with their shepherd, who played on a hair-thin flute. Butterflies.

My favorite animal, the only one Anita permitted me to touch, because it was not made of glass, was a Steif mouse with a button in its ear, soft and larger by far than the other creatures in the crystal world it seemed to have strayed into. It wore soft yellow felt slippers. I was not allowed to open the armoire and could play with the slippers only in the company of Anita, only to put the mouse back in its place immediately. Door closed. To annoy Anita, I ran around the round table in the middle of the room, so that the glass panes of the armoire trembled in their frames and one heard the glass sighs of the fragile glass society within.

On full-moon nights the menagerie played the light through tiny prisms. Opposite this armoire stood a terracotta stove, upheld on its two sides by two fauns, who impatiently wiggled their hoofed terracotta thighs. The light from the Nymphenburg porcelain candelabra in the middle of the room spilled across the wooden floor like a sigh. Whereupon, from the corner where my sister's bed stood, a sigh intruded into my half-dream, half-sleep. It sounded like sobbing. Then I saw her body at the window against the night sky. And there with her stood a silhouetted figure, laid a silhouette hand on her hair, her neck, bent over her and the two of them melted into a dark whole. Whispering. The figure separated and disappeared. Sleepily I saw through the glass menagerie how my sister tossed on a scarf and crept on tiptoes out of the room. Click went the door, and now, wide awake and bewildered about what it all meant, I saw her silhouette glide along the balcony that ran below our window, connecting the house with the stalls downstairs and the haystack upstairs.

I know something, I said the next day as Anita and Heinz combed the horses in front of the stables. Both looked up right away.

So what is it? said my sister, in an impatient tone which she mainly reserved for me. I was supposedly spoiled and got on her nerves.

What? they both asked now, grown curious because I did not want to come out with it straight off, instead taking a brush in my hand and starting to comb Bella's breast. No one else was in the courtyard. Now the two of them took the few steps across to me.

So what is it you know? Heinz asked amiably.

Now I could not hold it back any longer.

That you have been standing up here in the night! As I spoke I pointed to the balcony in front of our window.

Rubbish, said my sister cockily. But Heinz held my arm firmly, gently took the brush out of my hand.

Come, we're going to go over there, I have something to tell you.

We sat down on the green bench next to the stables. Heinz turned my shoulders so I could look directly into his face.

It's a secret I want to share with you, he smiled. No one is allowed to hear about it, not under any circumstances. I will be taking you with me into town every time I go, and sometimes even on my motorcycle, to go swimming. Very shortly. Anita will ride behind on Bella.

My sister stroked my hair.

That will be fantastic, she said with a new look of excitement.

Heinz pressed his finger across my lips and winked. Secret.

Ahh, now so many things changed. Now I had a sister, the kind I had always wished for. Now she listened to me when I told her my stories at great length. I was allowed to borrow her amber necklace for hours on end, could feel the gentle, light stones around my throat. I got to liberate first one then another of the glass animals from the armoire, too, hold it in my hand like a treasure until it got warm. Then another. Ahhhh.

As soon as Heinz was finished with his work on the farm and in the fields, he and Anita both saddled the horses. The animals needed exercise. They rode through the fruit trees, across the nearest meadow, further on across the stubbly harvested field, then a stretch of country road, over a little bridge, toward the forest, which like a broad charcoal stroke separated the land from the sky. My sister draped herself across the neck of her horse and galloped onward, with Heinz in hot pursuit. Free chunks of earth went flying up from their hooves. A terrified hare zigzagged out in front, a hawk grabbed a mouse and strove high up into the air. I watched them and could not wait until they returned, and I once again felt the power of our secret, which now encircled the three of us like a wall, keeping the others out.

And sometimes, when it was very hot, when the day had heated up like a tile stove, I rolled my woolen bathing suit into a towel and waited impatiently next to Heinz's motorbike, until he was finally at the point where he would let me on it. We raced up the road at unimaginable speed, the smell of dirt whirled about us, my hair tried to cling to my mouth, I clung to his body, the hot dusty air rushed by, the motor sang higher and higher like a circular saw. I was infinitely happy. And then, quite unexpectedly, the forest opened up and we had arrived at the lake.

Heinz switched off the shrill motorbike and leaned it on a tree stump. He spread out the blanket. I undressed ceremoniously beneath my dress and put on my bathing suit, which I hated so much, as it itched my skin. But Heinz thought it pretty, because it was red.

After a while one heard the tram, tram, tram of horses' hooves from the forest, and an instant later Anita stood before us. She dismounted, hot and happy. They embraced, with a fleeting kiss I was allowed to see as part of the Great Secret.

Watch the things, we're really headed into the water now. Later on I will take you on my shoulders, said Heinz cheerily.

Bella was tethered to a tree and flapped her tail at the flies. The motorcycle stood, leaning there. I slid down the embankment to the dark pond and looked for flat stones to send skipping across the water. Little slime farts. A cheeky dragonfly sat himself down on my thigh, frogs gaped through the mesh of water lilies. Swamp grass and rushes stood as masters of ceremony between me and the water out there. Suddenly, there was the splashing of a swamp thrush.

Floop! A fish sprang up to snatch a bug. Bees and bugs and swarms of mosquitoes. Something was creeping up on me. This was getting claustrophobic, there was too much of an uproar around me. Suddenly I could no longer bear being so alone in the heat.

Aaaannnnniiiiitttttaaaaaa! I screamed.

Heeeeeeiiiiinz! IIIItaaaaa! EEiiiinnz! came echoing back.

Heinz! Anita! I cried again.

I was standing up at the edge of the lake, by our blue-and-white blanket, using my hand to shield me from the light that glowed and pierced.

And, from far away, from the lake opposite, the answer came back, tired and hesitant: Just a minute, just a minute, we'll be there! Splashing, slaps on water, water rings that came nearer and nearer, and there was Heinz, finally surfacing. Come on, he laughed up from the water, and turned his broad back toward me so I could climb aboard.

Anita lay on the black swamp-water sky. She moved her arms only a little, so as not to sink. Her hair had seeped into the algae and floated sluggishly about her. We left her…

•

When we played which flower each family member should be, Anita was the peony, and I was columbine. What about Heinz, I asked? Iris, with the leaves a great saber, Anita answered, laughing.

"Class pretensions," Heinz had often said in a dismissive tone, when they discussed the parents, and my sister nodded and snuggled up to him. For her, Heinz was the cosmopolitan who had catapulted himself beyond the provincial thinking of my parents. Who had proven himself a strong man despite everything placed in his way. What a victory! They had their horses in common, the blue forest that adjoined the meadow, the sweet scent of hay, the poems, the motorbike with the wondrous velocity that balled up her skirt as they rode, whipped down her hair. They had one another.

One day Heinz asked my father for Anita's hand. Neither of them could keep the secret to themselves any longer. They were sure that it was time to share their happiness, that it would convince everyone. On the contrary. The parents, who

49

tried to bridge the social chasm between us and our workers with friendly sympathy, indeed with a genuine interest in their fates, were suddenly confused. The thought that someone from the working class would step so close to them was a blow that shattered their accustomed framework. It was completely unthinkable.

Whereupon everyone awoke from their Sleeping Beauty nap. Habitual assumptions no longer had any validity. Suddenly there were the most frightful scenes. Heinz was declared a murderer, an absolute villain, who had kidnapped, seduced, stolen one's daughter. No one even asked Anita, the object of the parental confusion, what her feelings were.

This upstart nobody posed as some kind of manager! my father bellowed senselessly into the room.

How could you get mixed up with this prole, child?! comes my mother's choked cry.

My sister sits on the bench that encloses the tiled stove, beneath which the dogs would otherwise be sleeping. But this uproar has sent them fleeing into the hall. Anita leans her head against the warmth of the oven. Her hands lie open in her lap. Tears run down her cheeks, ceaselessly, down the edge of her blouse. Leaning on his cane, my father limps to the window, to cool his brow on the glass. At his throat a bulging vein pulsates from a raging heart.

We gave that jerk every possible chance! Thus my mother's wail. In her helplessness she starts to cry.

I sit further off on a chair, confused. Just yesterday Heinz was with us at table, my father telling his stories. I know this chaos is tied up with our secret, its magic now lost. Heinz left the house an hour earlier, without saying goodbye, climbed onto his motorbike and drove off.

I hate Anita. I despise her, because she makes our strong mother so weak. That my mother is crying is terrifying to behold; her helplessness, her weakness, which I feel, is unbearable. I cry too, out of fear and confusion. We avoid looking at one another, and struggle for air as if we were suffocating.

My father moans, and we all look at him. He throws his cane into the room;

it hits the floor with a loud noise. He is about to burst with rage—nothing like the Fritz of yesterday at the dinner table.

My mother leaps up and hurls herself upon my sister like a hawk, slapping her across the face.

Don't go to that bastard! she cries. That prole! She spits the word out in disgust.

Adi's face has twisted itself into a grimace. She strikes Anita again, aimlessly, wherever the blow lands. My sister does not stir; only her form changes, with every blow. She ducks and pays the price of not giving up the price.

You must be polite and kind to all the people who work for us, my mother had always said. I had grown up in that spirit. But now she was repugnant to me. I did not understand her any more.

For a long time I held this scene inside me like a wound, as if I had been the one beaten. The cane on the wood floor, the sigh of the bench where my mother sat down in exhaustion, the sobs of the three of us and the stillness that followed, where one could hear the shrill buzzing of a fly in its death dance.

The truce had brought the dogs back into the room, going from one person to another to lick our hands. Emissaries of love.

•

My parents still lived in the time when they themselves had been young, in the unshatterable class consciousness that set limits. Only Max, my mother's father, had, when he was already a very old man, married his cook, who was very pretty and brought her wonderfully cute son with her into the marriage. The family had swallowed this "mistaken liaison," since Anni was uncommonly loving to Max, and he could not have cared less what others thought about him.

In the mirror of his helplessness, his powerlessness, the sinister idea came to my father of getting around the "matter" with money. Heinz had already been gone some time from our farm, and once again it was I who carried a secret about with me; for only I knew Heinz was still around. Anita wrote letters she shoved into her jacket pocket when she went riding.

My father also wrote a letter that turned him into an attorney and completely destroyed his dignity. He sat firmly screwed into his desk chair, the roll-top of the monstrous piece of furniture pushed back, so that it seemed even larger, and he himself looked small and stunned.

Come on, Fritzl! my mother urged, stroking his remaining hair. He answered with a groan, until morbid reflection made him burst out in a sweat, and he gave birth to the damnable idea of offering Heinz not just money but also a sea journey to America. Contingent on a declaration of renunciation, which Heinz was to sign.

In this oppressive interim Anita acted like an animal—a lethargic, dark snake that seemed to have made its way into an unsuitable climate, to which it was unable to adapt. She reduced herself to the barest necessities: Breath Light Bread Poop Sleep Sleep. And now she truly sobbed in her bed every night. When it woke me up, I saw through the glass the dancing prisms of the glass menagerie in the armoire and the twitching of Anita's body.

Should I bring you some water? I whispered. She did not answer, drew her pillow over her head, and the room became silent.

That was at night. But on some days one could also clearly see her other side, the powerful animal of love—a leopard that nourished itself on the helplessness of our parents. She spoke little, climbed onto her Bella and rode off.

My mother reclaimed her strength, and, as if to calm herself, she sighed out Cassandra warnings:

My God, that would never have worked! That much one can count on five fingers. A catastrophe. They had nothing in common. No family, nothing. That always goes wrong.

Our father no longer spoke much. His own volubility had betrayed him. He had swallowed the listener's bait, something that had never happened to him before. Heinz, whom he had valued so highly, whom one could rely on, had exploited him in the shabbiest imaginable way, crucified him. Fritz simply could not have dreamed that Heinz, who was fifteen years older than his daughter and brought nothing with him but a future that existed only courtesy of Fritz himself—that this creep would have the audacity even to cast a single glance at this beautiful, forbidden creature.

As the strength disappeared from my father's legs, he also felt his other powers dwindling.

Heinz, for his part, with the decisiveness of love, did not sign the letter of renunciation that was supposed to shove him off to America.

Hammer or Anvil

MY FATHER QUICKLY GREW OLD. His features irrevocable, his gaze astonished and critical, paired with the portentous emptiness of the cripple. He had only the Now, no future worth mentioning. Sometimes he laughed; then I ran to him straightaway.

Increasingly his sick legs prevented him from traveling the land that had claimed all his love, and slowly the illness killed even the wish. Our long family walks, proper wanderings, were now abbreviated, and he more often avoided them. His oblique humor bore sarcastic thorns. Remarks slipped from his lips, sharp and pessimistic.

Come on Fritzl, you don't really mean it! said my mother, and calmingly stroked him across his shoulder.

Fritz looked up angrily to the ceiling.

That's exactly what I do mean.

Adi, who was still very beautiful, whose face had not changed, laughed and took Fritz's black remarks as testimony to their opposite.

People always wanted to look at my mother. Her high forehead, her face the perfect oval of an Ingres portrait. Still framed by black hair, rolled up into a knot at her neck. Her body was strong, almost coarse, yet satisfied and in relaxed good health. She could hold everything at bay and everything together.

Often in families a theme is smothered in silence, because there is a general theory that this will put the matter to rest. In my family, we spoke no more about Heinz, but for a time the frightful arguments lurked in the rooms, the corridors, before falling silent en route to oblivion.

This was the period when my parents bought the car, the DKW cabriolet, and Adi, with her strong nerves, hurled herself onto the roads, which were still uncongested, since few people owned cars. Back in the trunk a canister of petrol always traveled along, for there were not many filling stations. We drove Anita in the "blue miracle" to Schloss Elmau, a hotel near Garmisch, and we actually arrived—noteworthy, since the Blue Wonder was full of technical glitches, which often left my mother on the shoulder, waving in despair at one of the autos that infrequently passed by. Often Adi would forget to top up the petrol canister in the trunk. The auto tours where everything went smoothly always stood out as special in our memory.

Anita was now nineteen years old and was to learn hotel management in the Schloss hotel at Elmau. Our parents had found this profession for her and she immediately agreed. She would have agreed to do a doctorate in janitorial science if it would get her away from home.

I remember an elated letter, even some photos, telling the story of a picnic in an alpine meadow, with a naked cliff tooth in the background, my ravishing sister in her dirndl, laughing; next to her, waving into the camera, a blonde student friend with her hand on her forehead, shielding her eyes against the sun.

On the picnic blanket, across the cake, the cups, across Anita's feet, stood the ominous shadow of the photographer.

And when my sister returned from her hotel training, which lasted half a year, she had grown up. She held her head high, chin forward. Her face had lost its softness. Her mouth, too, was decided, her gaze critical and somewhat bored. When one asked her something, she needed a little while to answer, as if she were surfacing from some other much more important world of thought.

Within the family, only the more straightforward things were discussed. And so it was the season of forgetting.

With me she had once again found the abrupt tone of an older sister. There were no more secrets to guard. Friendly was now superfluous.

On the windowsill, my throne, bleached by the morning sun, dead flies were scattered like black crumbs. Outside in the courtyard, Anita mounted her Bella. Up above, between the buildings, a little patch of blue sky. She turned Bella, clicked her tongue, and trotted out through the gate. The hooves thundered across the wooden planks. She was outside, free.

My mother wished very much that someone would take over the farm, take it off Fritz's hands. This wish had to be handled with a cool understanding and very little emotional expenditure. Heinz, whose competence would have made him the ideal candidate, had fallen out of the running.

My father stood in the middle of the courtyard, leaning on his cane. His brow was furrowed. Everywhere he saw impudence and disobedience. A bridle lying about. A hay wagon with a broken axle, simply forgotten there. Buckets that caught the water that streamed through the damaged roof on rainy days. Cattle that grazed through broken barbed-wire fences. Fewer and fewer chickens—these were gradually succumbing to friend fox, who grew ever bolder, dared enter the garden, where he manifested as a rust-red daub of color complacently strolling among the vegetables.

At first Fritz did not want to believe it. But as everything got worse and worse he was seized by impotent rage.

What is this goddamned chaos? he screamed into the courtyard. Does no one have eyes in their head?!

My long-alienated brother Uli shook his head over his father's abstruse fantasies. What did the parents still want here on the estate? He could not understand why the farm should be preserved. He also found the idea of a successor, supposedly assured by marrying Anita off to an agriculturist, completely cracked. The thought that somehow he, Uli, might run the farm struck him as absurd. He had married into a brewery that had made him rich, and my parents, happy. Now he visited us only occasionally with his wife and their three boys. It looked to me as if he came from the mainland to visit us on an island. And as if he had to hold a mirror up to this inside-out world to understand our parents.

•

In the kitchen there was an hourglass into which moisture had seeped. One had to tip it with one's finger or the sand would get stuck, and then one would think: now time is standing still.

But at some point, quite without grand gestures, without ceremony, silently, the way people manage it with great resolve, my sister's glass menagerie was carefully rolled up in cotton wool and newspaper, packed up in little boxes. I was allowed to help her. The glass armoire was disassembled into flat parts and two drawers. Then both our beds. The round table from the middle of the room, the sofa, two chairs, and the commode were brought downstairs. In the room next door, which looked northward, the skeleton of my grandmother's old bed filled up with a mattress and duvet for me to sleep. A dog slept in my room now, instead of my sister.

Anita took along everything my mother gave her.

Mountain landscapes painted by Grandfather. Five Piranesis. Her horse, the saddle, linens, Meissen crockery. Anita took along everything my mother gave her. She moved in with Heinz on a farm near Bamberg, where he was now the manager, as he had been with us. Adi could only think of one thing: how poor Anita would now be. So she slipped her all sorts of things. My sister seemed insatiable. This quality both women would forever retain in their relations with one another: indefatigable and insatiable.

The truck, piled up with furniture, baskets, and boxes stowed under the billowing tarps, pulled away. Mother, Anita, and I jumped into the Blue Wonder, to help with moving in. My father stayed behind, alone on the farm.

All the best to you, child, he had said as they left, kissing Anita on the fore-head as he spoke. He turned from us so that we would not be able to see his face, and pushed aside a stone with his cane. As he turned back to us again, he had recovered his composure. He was a man who did not easily display his feelings, his sentimental side, including his sorrow, although to emotions such as impa-tience and anger he gave free rein.

Resigned and exhausted by wishing for the ideal life he had thought out for her, he turned and went slowly to the lookout where he could see us and we him from a long, long ways off. My mother twisted around constantly in her seat so she would not lose sight of Fritz. One hand gripped the wheel; with her free hand, she waved. Anita stuck her head and arm out of the open window and stared back at Father, who melted ever further into the landscape.

I do not know whether he ever gave Anita his blessing.

A bit further, in the forest, Anita and my mother noticed that they had traded Fritz for the trees; they rolled up their windows. My sister leaned back with a long sigh and closed her eyes. She smiled, and it seemed as if she were extinguishing the dark times with the precision of an eraser.

•

I was an old child. I say this because I can clearly remember that at the age of ten I often knew, rather exactly, what was going on inside the people around me. Although one never spoke directly about money among us—that was simply not decent—I could sense, through allusions and scraps of conversation, that our fortune was slowly running out.

Indeed, the farm my father loved so much had to be sold.

Arriving at the uppermost stair on the upper floor of our ancient home, one found oneself looking into a gray mirror that had hung there for a very long time, witness to generations that had lived here before us. Longing, joy, hatred, shortcomings, love, death had filed past it. Time and moisture had contributed to the dissolution of the mirror surface into dust. Now it was blind. Silhouettes from out there—a section of roof, the clouds, treetops, and you yourself— stood shadowy in the silver-gray of a life-sized daguerreotype.

My father quoted Goethe:

Du musst steigen oder sinken,   *You must climb or sink,*
Du musst herrschen und gewinnen,   *You must rule and win,*
Oder dienen und verlieren,   *Or serve and lose,*
Leiden oder triumphieren,   *Suffer or triumph,*
Amboss oder Hammer sein.   *Be hammer or anvil.*

Anita was to be a hammer.

•

In a tiny farm chapel Anita waited for her marital blessing in front of the ornamented altar. Silent as a flower. She wore her saffron dress, the one with the birds of paradise. Next to her stood Heinz in a blue suit that hung on him as if he had borrowed it from a giant. Heinz— this he had in common with my father— was not made for sentimentality. So he spent the ceremony clinging to his stiff dignity.

My mother and I sat together with the aristocratic couple for whom Heinz now ran agricultural operations. They were smitten with Heinz's competence, just as my father had been. But they had seen through the situation here and were glad my sister was not their child. Just like my parents, they too would have wanted someone else for their daughter.

That Fritz had stayed home—that they understood.

My sister's happiness bathed the little baroque chapel in an otherworldly light. And, bathed in this light, the frescoes gleamed within their false perspectives, as did Lazarus with his far-too-large head. And it became an enchanted wedding party. Two lilac bouquets framed the couple like a gem of imperishability. My mother cried bitterly, as if it were a funeral, did not calm down until the ceremony was over and Baron Sachenbacher reached her his arm.

To celebrate, we went across to the castle, past the forgotten flower beds that encircled the little porter's house in which we had already laid out Anita's dowry. Heinz's motorbike with its sidecar was once again leaning in front of the door.

I too became a wild animal, once the time had come.

Part Two

She could not talk to them about her adventures. She made her decisions quietly, with the irrepressible will of a worthy lover.

The Letter-Writer

THE STENCH OF COLD SMOKE in the compartment of the train that brings her to a suburb. A crooked, mistrustful little grin is glued onto the face of the uniformed official who snips her ticket.

She has promised Ralf this visit. The two of them are following, chasing something neither of them can name. At first it was an idea, the spark of an ignition, but as they stroll through the little locality, whose foreign streets are sweating in the midday silence, and Ralf accidentally bumps her arm, she is startled.

'Scuse me, says Ralf.

Beneath a cherry tree the pavement is colored red by the mousse of crushed fruit; above them the threatening hum of a bee swarm. In the garden to their left and right blooms flax and foxglove. Above them stretches out the Bavarian sky, blue as never before.

I live there, Ralf says, gestures with his chin at some house, and turns off around the corner.

Against the fence leans a blue bicycle made for a man.

As they arrive at the last house in the village, the view opens onto a field across which, at regular intervals, grain bound up in the form of huts stands out to dry. They leave the path and walk across the stubble, diagonally across the vast field, toward the center. Behind one of the grain towers, where no one can see them, they lie down on the hard ground in the piercing midday sun. She looks about, squints toward the sky. High above her hovers a cloud in the form of a sheep.

The whistle of a returning train tears itself into little shreds above van Gogh's field. It seems that an eternity separates her from the village and the train station.

I have to get home, she shrieks, jumping up and racing across the tares, between the grain towers, crisscrossing to the path, flitting past the blue bicycle, a whirlwind of color, racing through the tree tunnel with the bee swarm, across the crushed cherries, feeling the grinding pebbles beneath her feet, panting wildly as she reaches the train station.

The train pulls in slowly, a grandiose spectacle of squealing brakes and clouds of steam. On the platform, easily recognizable by his crooked grin, stands the uniformed official who snipped her ticket on the way in.

Now he seems so familiar that she wishes he would climb aboard the train with her and accompany her home.

And from quite far away, from the fields on the outskirts of town, calls the cuckoo. Cuckoo, cuckoo, cuckoo...

•

It was an unexpectedly cold winter as I turned fourteen. I just had to wait until summer, then I would be finished with boarding school. In the school, Fräulein Sacher and Fräulein Meineke ruled over 120 interned girls, who, like me, lived too far away from Munich. Having grown up in the country, I felt as if I were in prison, but there was nothing that could be done. I absolutely had to go to this strict, refined school. It came complete with mandatory Latin lessons, which my father thought I had the brains for.

In the afternoons there was free time from one o'clock to four. It was winter, so we went in pairs, in groups of three or four, with skates slung over our shoulders, to the "Prinze." One slunk under the wooden planks of the stands, heard the loud blaring of the music, and already there was the *krrr* of the skates on the ice, producing expectant excitement within us like a noise machine countering the loud music. In the middle of the arena danced those who could dance well. The others, who were still practicing, or taking lessons, did exercises in the corners.

Clockwise! Keep it orderly or there will be consequences!—bellowed the voice from the loudspeaker when someone went against the stream.

I clambered up onto one of the spectator stands to pull on my skates. A birthday present. Previously I just had owned old-fashioned Dutch-style iron skates, metal screwed onto ski boots; the damned things were always coming loose and bending my ankles. Now, with the superb new white leather skates, I could really cut loose.

Should I help you put on your skates? A voice right next to me.

I looked up and laughed nervously. This is a fellow I have already seen here a few times, I thought, and extended a foot toward him.

Yes, if you like. Then I'll keep my gloves on.

Next to me the giggling began. My God, a boy had spoken to one of us. An electrifying vacuum took form around us, a total stillness. At boarding school we had been surrounded by only women for four years. When the gardener mowed the playing field behind the school, everyone noticed. Many girls opened windows and watched him, as if he were offering a fantastic pantomime.

The head with the woolen cap bent down and fished for the skates. Let them laugh, I thought, and drew back a little from the other girls.

I'm Kaspar, said Kaspar, and held my foot in his hand. With the other he undid the laces of my shoe to put the skate on me. He laughed like someone who has a plan, who has given things some thought, quietly and privately. I smiled, too, and left my feet in his care. When the shoes were laced, he led me into the ice arena.

With the new skates the skating went much better, and Kaspar called out to me encouragingly.

You can already skate quite well. I have seen it before.

From then on we met daily at the ice rink and whizzed around in a ring to warm ourselves up, and also because in the sheer excitement we did not know what to do other than get moving. At the same time we could touch each other. Words, even thoughts, were too fragile. Kaspar was already 18 and would be taking his finals in the summer.

Soon he was writing me at school, a love letter every day. Fräulein Sacher shook her head: yet another letter for you. I felt the heat of embarrassment as the hand holding the radioactive envelope shoved it across the table. Fräulein Sacher gave me a strict and hostile look, as if the number of received letters were a proof of a conspiracy against the virtue of the school.

As spring approached, Kaspar and I met on the way to my dance class at the Isadora Duncan School, in an ochre-colored villa in the Mauerkircherstrasse, surrounded by a little wall.

Sitting on the stoop, nestled together like two happy vagabonds, we forged a plan. We decided that from now on we would use various female names as senders, also different colorful envelopes. I was impressed by his airtight chess move. My thoughts swirled. Having Kaspar so near aroused me—the powerful lie even more so. When no one was looking, Kaspar pressed me to him and fumbled for my breasts. My hand, a weak attempt to moderate his storming of the fortress, was decidedly pushed aside. He covered every free patch of skin with an invasion of kisses. He called me his little she-goat and said he wanted more, more than these half hours in the ice cream shop, more than the all-too-brief encounters snuck in before and after my dancing lessons. More!

More? I did not know what to think. And so half of my brain, the deposed seat of reason, left the other a free hand.

When I was with Kaspar I felt a completely new helplessness, a kind of lameness that overpowered and entranced me at the same time, so that my will, otherwise so strong, yielded its place to a weak addict. I fished for something I could firmly hold onto, laughed nervously and noted details, like the lentils left behind in the fairy tale to show the way: a beetle with enameled tuxedo wings, how he worked his way up the stem; a blister from overly tight sneakers on the top of my bare toe; a crow, black, near the path, with an open beak, as if it wanted to call out something to me; my middle finger, blue from writing. I was almost struck dumb, as I did not want him to know how much I did not know, and nothing was to remind him that I was still a child.

In this diffuse state of mind Kaspar seemed more present than I did myself. He was obsessed with a particular idea, and nothing could hold him back from translating this idea into reality.

Kaspar wrote my parents a letter—purportedly in his mother's name:

Dear Mrs. Ost,

My daughter Petra has made friends with your daughter Beatrix, and with your permission I would very much like to invite her to spend next weekend with us. I live in the Berlinerstrasse, which is quite easy to reach with the #9 streetcar, in the same quarter as the school. My husband is a research physicist and unfortunately still detained by the Russians on Krim Island. So I live alone with Petra. We would very much enjoy a visit from Beatrix.

With warm greetings,

Margarete Busch

My mother was happy. I was to spend a weekend with the charming Petra. She wrote Fräulein Sacher that I was allowed to visit Frau Busch, an ersatz auntie, anytime. Adi was never mistrustful. She did not believe in lies. She would have felt it a waste of time to spy on her teenage daughter. She was firmly convinced of the goodness within every human being.

And so it came to pass that my good, clueless mother played the role allotted to her in the general melancholy of adolescence, when one phase of life has just ended and the other is just beginning. Had she had the slightest inkling, she would have turned into a beast in fear for me, and yet the huge, hard lie, shamefully red, flowed away and watered itself down in Kaspar's presence, a tender gray at first, until finally it existed no more.

Kaspar's father stared down from the wall next to the door of Kaspar's room, with a direct, questioning gaze. He had never returned home from the Crimea. He was in uniform and held his officer's cap firmly lodged beneath his arm. What little hair remained on his head had slipped down almost to his neck. Beneath the photo stood an old sofa, upholstered in pink damask. A moss-green army blanket was loosely tossed across the seat. This green blanket formed an air pocket between the cushion and the back, which called forth within me a sensation from my childhood: the canopy from my parents' open feather bed, into which I crept to hide as a child. In that narrow space, which only let in a little air, to which the eyes only slowly grew accustomed, I heard from afar my mother's voice calling, dampened by the featherbed. I could lie, say I had not heard her, and remain in my hiding-place until my own breath made it so unbearably hot that I would open the featherbed and thereby betray my whereabouts. Innocently, so to speak.

A scrap of light from the moon, assisted by the streetlamp, flowed across the little patch of carpet, across Kaspar's schoolbooks on the table in the center, across the clothes on the chair. We lay in his bed, quite silently, holding our breath. Smallest touches. With our fingertips we probed beneath the bedcover, in deaf-and-dumb language, gingerly, the length of our bodies, our legs tangled up in one another, our eyes closed. We scarcely dared breathe. So secret, so anonymous, without any familiar point of comparison.

In this room I was fourteen. First, hesitant contact with the transformation that awakens the beginning of a woman's life. I felt the welcome weight of Kaspar's body, which I already knew well from horsing around; with its taut muscles—now strengthened by his determination not to yield—to which I had already often succumbed. Plus a bouquet of the unfamiliar: the first serious smell of sweat from another skin, the tired scent of geraniums or elderberry flowers, of a man's semen. Scent of horse-chestnut tree blossoms. The language of the hands, whose gestures I permitted, which took in my whole body, stroked my sex, shared all five senses with me, faint with arousal.

I lay in bed with Kaspar, which, on the one hand overcame me, and which I nonetheless took with the composure and elegance of a child. I had entered a house where treasures were to be found.

Noticing my smallest movement Kaspar pressed me to him and asked concernedly: Are you all right?

In the middle of the room, to conceal the harsh, naked bulb, there hung, like a bat, a piece of netting, pulled across a wire mesh. Through the trembling prism of my eyelashes, insects electrified by the heat whirred like helicopters through the air, joined the dust on the pile of books, the coffee cup with its blonde milk ring, yesterday's buttered bread.

Outside in the corridor, in front of Kaspar's room, noises that I never forgot, that belonged to these four years, to this place, that never repeated themselves the same way. A key that worked its way into the lock, the click of the metal tumblers, the groaning of the dried-out hinges, the fall back into the catch.

Kaspar? A woman's voice.

Yes? answered Kaspar next to me. A moment of waiting, then steps which, accompanied by the creaking of the parquet floor, slowly lost themselves in the long hallway.

That was Kaspar's mother, whom he called Margarete, and who waved to me only once in these four years, as a silhouette against an open door, shrunk to a child at the end of the corridor.

The son of a widow. They had the discreet manners of an older married couple. The widow and the son. Sometimes he went out into the corridor after the "Kaspar?" and drew our door shut behind him. A page with another chapter. Silence outside. Dumb lips in an undescribed face gesticulated through my breathless listening, dramatized. The wall remained impermeable, until the steps creaked their way along the hall and Kaspar, back in the room, doorknob in his hand, caused the only sound: Click.

In those four years, in this room, I grew up next to Kaspar. Often I dreamed the same dream, which grasped for me with long, thin fingers:

My father, in his duster, buttoned up all the way, takes his leave, climbs into the coach that will bring him to prison. It is because of the illicit slaughter of animals.

I stand with my mother in front of the house. We wave. On the farm we had so many mouths to feed and the official rations were insufficient.

He returns with Umer, the coachman... I see my father's triumphant face and I am glad...

I dreamed this realistic dream because my father had lied his way out of prison. I knew this because there was talk about how easy it was to convince the stupid police with lies. I, too, had lied, and through this swindle had always returned to this room with ease.

I love you, said Kaspar. I nodded. We said that to one another often in this room. And from this sunny morning on, I saw many times, outside, between this house and the next, a patch of sky. A glass atop a heap of books. A ray of sunlight that shot through a prism and threw diamonds onto the little table. I heard a dark clock ringing the hour from not too far away. One, two, three, four. Then one, two, three, four, five, six, seven: a shriller bell. There followed a piece of music from the chorus of bells. Propped up on my elbow, I pondered the face of the boy next to me. Kaspar, with whom I would have eloped in an instant, was fast asleep. His straight nose had a light curvature upward at the tip. Beneath it spread out on both sides, evenly, a thin carpet of tiny blond hairs that framed the soft, large mouth. Without the wings of his will flapping at all, the breath went in and out, sank and arched his brown breast. Behind the closed lids the eyes moved as if pictures, drawn by invisible threads, were marching past in procession. Above his head, half covered by the smooth blond hair, his open hand lay outspread—held an invisible ball.

•

I am in Munich for a visit. Let's see: Does my first love, Kaspar, still exist? I find his number in the telephone book. On the one hand I want to see him, on the other, to ask for permission to write about him. I immediately recognize his voice through the phone. The World Cup roars in the background.

Sure, drop by, I'm home, he says laughingly, as if we had just seen one another, as if the fifty years gone by since we parted did not exist.

On the way to his apartment, I am full of nostalgic expectation.

Kaspar holds the door open for me with a friendly smile. I feel a time machine carrying me back. Back where we opened the door to the world together. Time seems merely to have grazed him. The only thing that has changed about his mane is the color, silvery gray. His movements, too, are the same, just a bit slower. His apartment, through which he leads me, is similar to his earlier student housing, but with several rooms.

Kaspar is quite matter-of-fact, not astounded at my sudden appearance. He tells me about his present life, tells me also that his third wife is twenty years younger than he. At this he gives a satisfied laugh.

I'm writing a second book, I tell him. Stories about myself...You were my first love, you know.

Is that so? he replies with a friendly laugh. I have to laugh with him—so typically male, the way he shields himself from allowing any feeling of nostalgia to come to the surface, while I carry the sweet past within me.

He shows me a photograph.

Those are my three boys, from three marriages.

I hold the photo in my hand for a long time. Kaspar and his sons look the same age.

The soccer match has his attention again.

Have fun, he says, and gives me a goodbye kiss. Send me the book when it's done.

•

My parents sold the estate and moved into the city. I was not living at boarding school any more. Our apartment overlooked the superb English Garden, and there, in the confusing labyrinth of paths and roadways, Kaspar meandered about with me, on the lookout for crannies suitable for making out. We hid under groups of trees, in leafy rooms, to wait with pounding hearts until a bundle of steps and a splash of voices went by our love nest, and we had the sighing of the trees and the intimate conversations of the birds to ourselves once again.

Fritz now needed Adi completely for himself. Their life had shrunk greatly, and his illness seized center stage. It nourished itself on what was still healthy.

My mother had the hasty stride of a young woman who cannot leave her child alone. At the butcher's she slowed down the pace. A treat for your fine husband, said the red-cheeked woman behind the counter, reaching across with a little piece of dewlap or kidney. Quite fresh—will this do? Fritz still had his privileges. The connoisseur. As he did back then on our farm, when I was a child and permitted to sit next to him when he got his daily eleven o'clock "meat treat", served on a wooden plate, and he fed me little pieces of meat impaled on the point of his knife. Then a chunk flying in a high arc through the room, for the dogs, who threw themselves on it like junkies and then immediately resumed their total veneration of their master, following the meat from plate to mouth with the back and forth of their heads.

But now I really must go, said my mother and hurried out of the shop to the vegetable stand. And while the fruits, the spinach, the carrots were weighed and packed up, she bought the newspaper. You could read the daily rituals, duty and love in all her doings. Adi was selfless, and joyous, quite simply a glad disposition, quite free on her own.

I see my father, one side propped on my mother's arm, the other holding itself up on his cane, going along Leopoldstrasse to the Siegestor. The same cane that had previously accompanied him across his broad lands, his fields, with which he had pointed and indicated, lately neglected tasks for the most part— that cane now led him along the narrow pavement, through the noise of civilization. Often they came to a stop, not because of the scent of the season, which Fritz had always celebrated with deep inhalation on his land. No. Now they stopped to let everything go by: things familiar, things strange, transient prisms registered from the side, animated bystanders, lips struck dumb, moving in foreign languages, dipping in and out of light and shadow, heartbeats interchanging, transformed energy, the absolute and the possible.

Adi looked upward at the poplars that lined the sidewalk, evidently planted immediately after the war, given that they grew so fast. High above she saw two quarreling sparrows flit in and out among the silver flutterings of the leaves. Fritz briefly had to catch his breath. Adi did not wish to notice his handicap, which led quickly to exhaustion, which in turn enraged him. She gave him time, until he had collected himself enough to go on.

Yes, the daily rituals of my parents, forced into the corset of love and duty, filled the days in the city: these rituals were no longer reminiscent of country life at all. In fact my parents had moved into the city to be as close as possible to the illness, or the cure, or the impossibility of a recuperation. With this complete alteration of their previous country life, they now lived an endless farewell.

Nothing could replace the old with the new. They were strangers in the city and strangers in my life.

The visits to friends and the earlier country neighbors became ceremonial.

Ah, how superb, the landscape! cried Adi, as if she were seeing the green hills thronging in front of the mountain chain for the first time. They toured through the familiar, dearly beloved country panorama and celebrated continually recurring farewells. Fritz, full of suppressed melancholy and impatience; Adi, brave and high-spirited. She never let anything show. She held on tightly to what was still there and had her wonderful optimism, which struggled with crass reality but always kept the upper hand.

My life arched like a rainbow above my parents' city existence. I found my parents old-fashioned, their views naïve. The tact my father required gave me a way to slip out into freedom. I needed nothing from them at all. Our daily routines scarcely touched. I made the decisions of an adult, which I then presented to my parents so casually, with so much dignity, that they never doubted my cleverness.

Beatrix is low-maintenance, I heard them say.

Black and White

I HAD BEEN APPROACHED ON LEOPOLD STREET by a fashion photographer. So it began. Even in schoolgirl days I went to photo shoots and played hooky to act in films.

I remember a trip to the highest peak in Germany, the Zugspitze. Winter outfits. A blizzard put an end to the project. A car trip to the Gardersee to photograph summer fashion, during which the fat hotelier, to universal laughter, proposed marriage to me. Commercials where I lauded washing machines; auditioning as a television announcer, a job for which I proved still too young. Later on, wonderful jaunts to Florence, where the fashionable world gathered in those days: the red-haired Suzi Parker; China Machado, with a shock of white in her black hair; Bettina, whom the playboy Rubi Rosa picked up in a Ferrari.

And although this variety of independence was alien to my parents, and on the one hand they did not really understand it so well, on the other hand they admired the sort of cleverness that meant I always had money.

•

My black-and-white spotted dog on the leash, I in an elegant and for that time unthinkably luxurious white leather coat with a black fur collar…High snowdrifts covered the city. Cars thronged the streets like sheep. A few hours earlier Bobsi Orentschuck had picked me up at home. Since he was older I was allowed to go to lunch with him, but not late in the evening.

My mother stood at the door for another moment. Her eyes followed us down the hall. The lower half of her face, the rest of her figure, dissolved into an indeterminate pink kaleidoscope. She could not have waved to us even if she wanted to.

Bobsi Orentschuck, in whose face the features melted into one another, where the big nose did not want to fit in, the rather too-large head, which in turn did not fit the short stature—Bobsi Orentschuck was a pretender. He wanted to leave a particularly strong impression with my mother. I knew she was laughing herself sick behind the gigantic rose bouquet there at the door.

What sort of girl was I back then, for Bobsi Orentschuck, so much older, to be so fascinated with me, to besiege me for weeks on end? I sewed my own clothes, hoop skirts in every color, made of felt. For a belt I would tie one of my father's neckties about my waist. I wore ballet shoes on the street. Flaming red lipstick. I had bobbed my hair à la Louise Brooks.

She is pretty—Beatrix is amusing—She has charm too, said my family. My father said: You are too conspicuous. It was perhaps because I was forever rein-venting myself. Creativity born from the lack of superfluities. I remember a gray slip manufactured by Bleyle, which gave me a terrible itch, but which, because of its color, I wore wrapped about my head as a turban.

At lunch, in the stiff surroundings of the fine restaurant Boettner, its name synonymous with money, Bobsi and I sat in the middle of the room so that every-one could see us. I understood almost none of the luxurious listings on the menu, and sat there next to Bobsi as the symbol of everything he tried to project. I ate as much as I could of the treats he had picked out, thinking to myself: Tank up!

Marilyn Monroe once said in a similar context: It's often enough to be with someone. I don't need to touch them, not even talk.

In the commercial streets of the city still heavily scarred by the war, burned-out stores still stood boarded up, like decayed teeth. Improvised barracks exuded the smell of sausages. Smoke climbed from a pipe on the tin roof. Many pathetically patched-up front doors. On the dirty house walls one still saw the arrows pointing down to an air-raid shelter. And yet, next to the misery reminis-cent of war was the other extreme: luxury as we had never known it.

No, not yet, please, said Bobsi O. He did not want to part from me yet. We turned off onto the Briennerstrasse, which had already regained something of the old luxury. Suddenly we were standing in front of Mencke, the fine, expensive boutique.

I stared at an incredibly elegant mannequin in the display window. In the mirror of her black coat collar I smiled at myself. The doll lifted her gloved hand. Come in, she waved.

Do you like it, asked Humbert Humbert Bobsi O.

I turned from the mirror.

I'll keep the coat on, I said to the saleslady.

It suits you better than anyone, she said.

Bobsi brought up the rear, carrying the package that now held my well-worn Loden cape. I did not walk, did not run, no, I glided along the white runway, toward the lions, pushed off their pedestals during the war, their dignity not yet recovered, lying in the rubble in front of the Feldherrnhalle. Through the condensation from my breath, I laughed and flirted with the people approaching, without seeing them, the white leather exterior of my coat soft as milk, on the inside the little black furs that embraced my body with tender intimacy.

I had long since forgotten Bobsi Orentschuck. I was impatient. I thought only of walking home, to show my face, to show my father. Papa, it's me, Electra!

Suddenly, without warning, close by, a loud bang. Shrill, deafening cacophony of steel and tin. A car raced through the wall of snow onto the pavement, toward the shop windows. Screeching people sprang apart looking for cover. My dog barked into the chaos as if he had gone mad. Wearing outraged, incredulous expressions, the people stared at the completely mangled vehicle, through the door of which a man was laboriously peeling himself. This tumult had crashed into the orderly pavement like a lightning bolt, and in no time at all had swollen into an avalanche of gaping idlers, Bobsi and I and my bellowing dog drawn willy-nilly into their midst, where we heard first in whispers, then loudly and clearly, that I was the guilty party.

It's hurr fawlt.

Cuz she's dressed so uppity.

Driver ain't seen it comin'.

Jus black'n white. Dog did its bit too.

Shameless. So outrageous.

That's the new youth for you.

All at once everything was moving in slow motion. Voices cut into one another. Disapproving grimaces moved in on me. Thirty pairs of eyes, or more, danced around me with expectant glee. The sidewalk, just a moment earlier moved by pounding hearts in lazy expectation, broke into pandemonium with the cracking of a nut. The serpent of envy throttled the joy at my luxury into horror. I felt as if my dream coat were being ripped from my body with greedy looks. And now I saw the filthy city snow in the gutter flowing together into a gray rivulet, I saw the irritable gray faces, their netted shopping bags with the most indispensable supplies wrapped in gray. I ran, I sprinted across the provisional wooden bridges over the potholes, hotly pursued by the chorus of loud accusation and the applause in the disapproving glances.

Finally, finally we found ourselves in the sheltering taxi where I noticed my completely drenched shoes for the first time. Bobsi hurled himself back into the seat and laughed so hard he could scarcely catch his breath.

"Cuz she's dressed so uppity…That's the new youth for you…and that coat…" HaHaHa! He doubled over with laughter. For him the scene was quite an amusing episode. Years later he still dredged it up for any listener he was trying to please.

The story became a blossom in the buttonhole of his vanity.

At home, as I recounted my adventure, my father looked up only briefly from his book. Even though the room had grown far too warm, I would not let go of my black-and-white trophy of fine leather, lined with silky soft mole fur. This piece of luxury constituted a symbol. I did not want to part with it.

My mother listened in amusement, while her facial expression echoed the story in pantomime. Astonished, she lifts her eyebrows. Mildly amused, her mouth closed to an upward-turned grin. Amid the apparent impassivity of my father, the kettle whistled from the kitchen, and with this my mother and I noticed that only the two of us were listening to one another.

Papa, do look, it's so beautiful and elegant!

He peered fleetingly and darkly away from his book, above the frame of his glasses.

You are to return the coat to Mr. Whatshisname. One does not accept such a present. Something is always demanded in return.

How could he understand? I thought to myself. Here, too, I made my decision quietly, with an irrepressible strength of will. I turned slowly and left the room.

Cosmic synchronicity had assigned Bobsi Orentschuck another role to come. But before that, I was not to see him again for many years, thus proving that there are presents, even large presents, that are weightless, light. Not even a kiss. Years later it would be Bobsi Orentschuck who was to give me a great present that hid within it one still greater.

When my father was feeling well amid his circle of friends who passed the time telling stories, he would lean back with the mien of a thought collector, the eyes lazy, half-closed, as if he were telling an ancient story.

That Beatrix, he would say slowly, that one is shrewd. She has a cool, calculating mind. No one can pull the wool over her eyes. The fellow who gave her the coat is just another example. Cool head. And as he said it, he tapped his forehead.

Coffeehouse Culture

OVER AND AGAIN, quite unhoped-for, my brother Uli popped up at my parents' place. Uli, fifteen years older than I, who had worries about me that my parents couldn't even imagine in their worst dreams: among many other things, worries about my ten o'clock curfew. Curfew was a concept not marked on anyone's wristwatch in those days. The hours before ten were also perfectly good for gaily trading secrets under chestnut trees, making friends beneath the table with a hundred barefoot nudges.

Kaspar stood at the door to pick me up, a mere lad, politely kissing Mother's hand with the face of a trusting angel. Narrow-shouldered, thin and a little awkward, he waited patiently in the downstairs hall until I had stuffed four petticoats under my skirt, belted my waist to 50 centimeters, put on my ballet shoes, wound ribbons round my ankles, daubed my mouth with the fiery red Revlon lipstick Fire on Ice. All that went very quickly, in order to rock out of the house in the shortest possible time. It was still high afternoon. But the precise preparations were for the nighttime that waited for Kaspar and me as the magpie waits for everything that glitters.

Scarcely had we turned the corner when we became grownups. Kaspar pressed me into a doorway and his hand deciphered the size of my bosom between foam rubber and skin. We walked to the Rialto. There the party began with the first postwar ice cream from Italy, with cappuccino and Campari. A seemingly endless procession—film producers; forgers; princes, authentic and otherwise, whom we called borderline aristocrats; actors; shooting stars of film; Nazi war criminals; photographers; connoisseurs and the spectacularly beautiful long-legged "Fräuleinwunder," thus dubbed by Playboy writer Franz

Spelman—all of them swarmed the pavements around the little tables, interrupted by Casanova waiters in black and white, trays high above their heads. Rumors wound their way about the legs of chairs. *Bonjour Tristesse* hung in the air. Promises and fantastic plans were bandied about.

Across the way sat Erich Kästner at his usual table, writing in his notebook: *The months are in a hurry. The years are in even more of a hurry. And the decades are in the biggest hurry of all. Only memories have patience with us. Particularly when we have patience with them.* His childhood reminiscences would soon be appearing: *When I Was a Little Boy, 1907–14 in Dresden.*

Erich Kästner looked over at us, smiled and waved. We were to join him at his table as an inspiration. He regarded us all the while with thoroughly kind eyes, peering forth from beneath the most sinister of Groucho Marx brows, whose wild profusion would have made one imagine them on a much taller and statelier man.

Vico von Bülow, who had emigrated from Prussia to Bavaria, his pen name Loriot, sat further away in front of his brandy and eyed the colorful society with the greatest amusement. In between he drew his satirical cartoons for the *Muenchener Merkur*, looked across at me and blew me a kiss. I found it incredibly exciting to be not just acknowledged by Loriot, the much older charmer, but indeed sometimes even challenged to take a seat over at his table, where the connoisseurs gathered. They conversed in a jargon I scarcely grasped, which made the encounter even more exotic for me.

Kaspar sat close by my side, wordless and kind, a sort of extension of myself. His presence made me feel protected from the onslaught of this new scene.

Among the scintillating, the authentic, the fakes, Siggi Sommer, whose *nom de plume* was Blasius der Spaziergaenger, kept an eye out for "moths"—beautiful, audacious girls. He would pin them into his newspaper column, deflating them with the ether of his observations. His novel *And No One Weeps for Me*, in which his heroine Marilli Kosemund sniffs the warm skin of her arm while watching the lads go wild, became my favorite book.

It was a seemingly endless procession of irresistible novelties: foreign languages and dialects that domesticated themselves, new music that we immediately grasped as an ambassador. Dschupp, Dschupp, Dschupp, Doo Doo Doo Wah, Do Wah.

As a fixed point in one of the cafes sat a Marilyn Monroe, her Bavarian interpretation an optical amalgamation. A living mannequin. Men eyed down into her décolletage, grinning impudently, to have themselves photographed. Marilyn changed her static position on the coffeehouse chair, stood up, bent forward, both hands steadied on her thighs, pressed her breasts together and laughed. A little breeze blew through her blonde hair, and everyone gaped.

Naturally the sun played an important role in this production. Marilyn needed droplets of light and good moods to lend her mirror image to robust reality. No one asked what she got up to on rainy days. She was a successful illusion, and that was enough.

At a small table in another café, in his own territory, resided Captain Hook, the one-armed tennis instructor. To intensify still further the open secret of his persona, he wore a black patch beneath his Brylcreemed forelock, over his left eye. A breeze of melancholy fanned about him. He was silent, like the cowboys in the new John Wayne films, who ride off alone into the infinite prairie. His right arm ended in a hook, in which he perpetually held a conical glass of Campari. How did he come to be missing this arm? everyone wanted to know. Not in the war. He was not such a fool as to have taken part. He was said to have been in Alaska, on one of his adventures, driving behind a truck laden with tree trunks. One of the trunks supposedly came loose and shot through his windscreen. With the loss of his arm the possibilities of another member were said to have soared into adventurous realms. All the women were apparently thinking the same thing and were enthusiastically passing one another within his revolving door.

Under the silent pretense of having to give a tennis lesson, he would leave the café. He never paid. A banal aspect of his carefully staged ceremony, one with which he never troubled himself. It would be settled by one of his adoring group-ies in compensation for other services.

With his stool in the one hand and the case with his brushes in the other, a shoeshine boy made the rounds and spat, cursing, on our shoes, which was sup-posed to enhance the gleam, but often missed the mark.

A-bend-zeitung! Münch-ner-Mer-kur! Süd-deut-sche! cried out the newspa-per man further down the sidewalk.

Ah, there she is, the Queen of Sheba! Johannes, Prince of Thurn and Taxis, called out gaily across the tables when he saw me. My cheeks turned red from so much center stage, and at the same time I enjoyed it, could not get enough of all that loud, sweet attention. We rolled with laughter at his worldly gossip, the latest. The hostess, Madame Ambassador Wally Styler, whom Johannes called a fossil, sauntered with him, arm in arm, excitedly chattering, directly into the swimming pool. She was quite stout and had to be fished out by a number of servants. But Johannes, dripping wet, took a deep bow and apologized. He was just so fascinated by her conversation. On top of his incredible sarcasm he could play the hypocrite with great charm and credibility.

Johannes was at once the most amusing and the most ill-mannered in this Who's Who Central of rumors, anecdotes, smutty tales, and everything noteworthy, which meant everything to us then and nothing today.

And everywhere, including in Schwabing, the artist's quarter, one would for many years walk through trashed streets, bump into boarded-up, burned-out houses awaiting resurrection. Dirty shreds of curtain fluttered from crooked window holes, grass grew through cracks in stairways, mountains of scrap loomed in front gardens with forget-me-nots. And when it rained, the legend of a street accumulated in the clogged gutters.

I was now a student at the Academy of Art. The Jugendstil villa I passed daily on my way there, beneath whose roof the most colorful frescoes told the story of Juno and the bull—this, too, bereft of owners, awaited its future destiny.

On many a night it was as if music were swelling through the leaded windows, down to the cypresses, where a woman was said to have plunged to her death while the Nazis were having a wild party.

There, in summertime, in the garden, between the gravel paths, in forgotten flowerbeds, bloomed pink peonies, blue foxglove, white irises, half suffocated by unrestrained vines. Rhododendrons pressed their way up the stone steps. I squeezed through the tattered fence and picked a garland. It was unnerving in the formerly feudal garden, and I looked up to see whether there was not someone staring down upon me from a window.

•

In the generation sandwiched between my father's and my own, there were drunkards like fishes. It seemed as if every corner in Schwabing boasted a filling bar. Whoever could think of nothing better, or thought of too many better things, had enough reason to permit himself a few glasses even in the early afternoon—or to give himself entirely free rein. A sort of collective exhalation, which seemed to harmonize with the collective heartbeat. Much of it had to do with the vacuum the war had torn into a generation, and many people had more on their back than their shadow.

•

Predestination wearing the mask of coincidence.

I first saw Him beneath the striped awnings, at Käfer's fruit stand, which had the lure of a casino. Starting at midday, after the housewives had gone shopping for their vegetables, men swarmed like wasps on a mountain of grapes around the potatoes, cabbages, kohlrabi, carrots, leeks, apples. For there, directly adjacent, beneath a cozy restaurant parasol, there piled up sausage and fish rolls, produced as if on an assembly line by Gert Käfer's mother, Sausage Resi. All fresh, just before the last remaining rolls were eaten. With it schnapps, wine, champagne, beer.

With small, attentive fox eyes she kept a tight watch on her threefold source of income. Nothing escaped the tiny, energetic woman with the commando power of a field marshal. On the right side, fruit that had to be weighed on a hand scale and packed up; on the left, eating the fish and sausage rolls, horsing around, consuming liquor and champagne, the constantly shifting squad of alcoholics, time bandits, bullshitters, car dealers, actors killing time, posers, sheep thieves, uninspired poets, and often enough, in their midst, a naughty beauty one could grab by the bottom.

There I saw Him for the first time, and afterwards I often noticed him, whenever I went past the place on my way to the Academy, so I came to remember him: the handsome hand, with a lion carved into a lapis ring, holding a schnapps glass; the brown locks of hair, the Clark Gable profile, the grinning mouth, medium height, laid-back, angular, with eyes like broken glass, though these he had in common with all the others who turned their head when I went by. He would hiss *"muy guapa"*, loudly enough for me to hear, laughing as he made me flush hotly. I knew immediately it was meant for me.

He always had a pipe in the corner of his mouth. All the men standing around there gaped at me, and I found it superb. Sometimes I would stop at the fruit stand myself and have a sausage roll. I could brave the throng my presence caused because I saw most of the men there every day and could thus recognize them, and they, me.

Right away one of the regulars called out: I'll pay for the lady's sausage roll! My treat! Would you like something to drink? Resi, got a lemonade? Whereupon the mens' club burst out in much-too-loud laughter.

I saw him there out of the corner of my eye; I could not really look; I just could not. I cast a sideward glance at his pipe ritual, for as long as he was busy with it. Scrape clean, blow, refill, tap tight and refill more, draw the flame into the bowl.

I chewed on my roll and the virtuosity of the drunkards in tossing everything down their throats, everything joyful and everything unpleasant, too, gave me the excuse for a brief moment of contemplation.

The Villa

BETWEEN THE END OF THE DAY and the petticoat of night, Kaspar and I visited an improvised, thrown-together cinema near the Nikolaiplatz. In the films they ran there, we recognized ourselves in every episode. *Le jour se lève* with Arletty and Jean Gabin. *Children of Paradise* with Arletty and Jean-Louis Barrault. De Sica's *Bicycle Thief.* Someone would tickle the keys of an old, scratched-up piano before the film began, singing:

Es ist ja ganz gleich, wen wir lieben	*It's all the same whom we love,*
Und wer uns das Herz einmal bricht	*And who ends up breaking our hearts;*
Wir werden vom Schicksal getrieben,	*We're driven by fate,*
Und das Ende ist immer Verzicht...	*And it always ends up a write-off*

We ate Hershey's chocolate, chewed Wrigley's gum, made out, and whispered through the Week In Review until someone complained: Sshhhh, Putta Lid Onit! And right then we remembered the other, actual reason why we had come.

The villa first surfaced in a chaotic dream sequence. I dreamed wild dreams back then, as I was drawn together with Kaspar into a world I kept hidden from my parents.

The figure of my father, screwed into his high-backed armchair at the window. Outside, a symmetrical wall of evergreens, like witnesses. My mother's dark hair, parted in the middle; she is young, younger than the woman I know. She must have climbed out of an earlier photograph, as she is wearing a familiar yet unknown gray dress, gathered at the breast. She bends over my father's shoulder. I see him in profile. The dress has countless round buttons that hop down the middle of its back. In the dream I wonder who could do up all these buttonhooks for her. Not Fritz, who can scarcely hold his fork any more... Adi tries to read to him from a newspaper article he will not give up, holds firmly with both hands, his fingers so cramped that the knuckles are white, and Adi must crook her neck to read better, Fritz cannot decipher it himself, as the print is too small, but on account of his handicap he does not want to go to the eye doctor. Yet in the dream it becomes clear to him that he would like to live a bit longer, not put it off any more; he says it would be worth it after all to replace the old glasses with new ones. Now he puts on these new glasses, which magnify—so gigantically that it makes him dizzy—the letters of a scandalous article set in a half-bombed-out Villa on Leopoldstrasse that belongs to Herr Aike.

Adi, you read it, he says and gives her the paper.

And then my big brother, Uli, surfaces from the microcosm of heaped-up snapshots, and as he appears, I wake up, and I know it is from fright.

"At Aike's" there were always parties. A villa harshly affected by the war. Crumbled and badly trashed, it was no longer good for anything else; once this postwar period was over, it would not be good even for this. Outside, in front of the entrance, danced a magical fire, around which Kaspar and I jostled with the others, red heat in our faces borrowed from the glow. The wind tore the smoke into shreds. From within, blues tones glided through the windows, thick and sweet as honey, with an irresistible fleshliness, as Billie Holiday sang:

I'll be seeing you
In all the old familiar places
That this heart of mine embraces.
—duduu, duduu, tschutschutschu—

Trampling of feet on the stair to the second floor, only up to the landing. Behind it the house suddenly broke off and married the garden. Undergrowth, left to wind in on itself for years, had grown into an impenetrable barricade, which replaced the wall of the house. If one stepped through the gate into the twilight, as soon as the eye adjusted, one could see couples intertwined on mattresses in the corners. Lace woven from paper streamers hung as a fragile canopy at the ceiling. Beneath it were slashed, worn-out sofas, fruit crates taking the place of tables, moth-eaten Persian rugs covering the holes in the floors. Diffuse flickers from candles stuck onto wax stalagmites.

Once we had pushed forward into the inner sanctum, shoved, pressed, pulled, woven about with cigarette fog, most of our senses left us. We became creatures of the demimonde, a sort of cult that the postwar hunger for freedom had reinvented. This was round about 1956. Perhaps. Vast quantities of beer, schnapps, and cheap Chianti belonged to everyone who had paid his oblation—as much as he wanted. We insisted on our new jazz music, loud discussions, fraternization, jealous scenes, sensual tendernesses, and asserted a regal right to disobey.

Under grubby blankets, in corners, couples forgave one another their infidelities. Between wine bottles, puddles of beer, glasses stuffed full of cigarette ends stood a bouquet of poppies, their blossoms loud and red, their consistency tender, like butterfly wings—stood there like an X-ray of our collective soul. A longing, something lost, made us cling to what we had found in this ruin. Nothing for the petit bourgeois. A rebellion, lusty disorder, on the slope between appetite and prohibition. It vibrated like china on a tray—only we knew the secret code, which we did not cast doubt upon with unnecessary questions. The music slunk like a cat up the wobbly stairs, lay down with the lovers on the fragile landing, hovered amid the spiders' webs, sighed out into the thicket behind the midnight house.

Against the sulfurous light through the doorframe, figures moved about, drawn on by the rhythm of the music. They wore jeans that they seemed soldered into. One arrived at this formidable silhouette by climbing, with the jeans, into a piping hot bath, then letting them dry on one's body.

Once again, obtaining blue jeans—which fit us now like the dirndl and lederhosen in the Bavarian Lower Alps—was part of the tricky dependency dynamic of Who Knows Whom. Who had an American friend in the PX? The hotly desired jeans not only reflected the picture of fashion, but also interpreted a body language as the Zeitgeist.

Loud thronging, laughing and shoving, men and women with glass-shard eyes, and there, by the beer keg and the cheap Chianti bar, with a bottle in his handsome be-ringed hand, balancing his pipe in the corner of his mouth, leaned the one I already knew, the one I did not trust myself to look at straight on, the one I could look at only out of the corner of my eye, as if I were interested in anything but him. He was in the middle of giving a talk that the women, and the men too, listened to, smiling excitedly. Verbal scraps drifted across to me.

Adventure...I always have to move on...it hems me in...the gods are calling me...we're on the same page...the heavens belong to us both...

Movie-star grin. He took the pipe from his mouth and, while he told some choice tales, he played out the pipe ritual: blow through, fill, compress with a silver instrument, wooden match, suck the flame into the bowl. He continued:

As soon as you set foot on Mexican soil, you are playing by different rules: best to stick a banknote beneath your passport when you hand it to the customs officer...

I watched. From beneath his impudent brown locks he ogled the girls. *Surabaya-Johnny...Take that damned pipe out of your mouth, you dog.*

The clock pealed the hours. Hoopla! I remembered my curfew, which had been running along far behind me for quite some time, out of breath.

A nervous rain had begun to fall, and outside the front door the fire pit had accumulated into a lake, across which Kaspar had to lug me. Shoes in hand, we stumbled through white ribbons onto the street. Before us tumbled headlights, soft and sketched, as if on a faded photograph. We used the puddles, into which the lanterns bended, as mirrors; lifted our heads and drank in the rain like doves. Icy rivulets tickled their way down our throats, collected between my breasts. I sang:

> *I'll be seeing you*
> *In Aike's old familiar places.*
> *—I'm not going home tonight—*
> *The whole night through.*

Kaspar, my magician, laughed madly. From his mouth sprang rays of light, little snakes.

*Now since my baby left me, I've found a new place to dwell...*Finally we landed in front of my door, barefoot, shoes in hand, Elvis's *Heartbreak Hotel*, and down poured the rain. I rummaged for my keys, keys. Kaspar wrung the rain out of my shoulder bag and we laughed, laughed, and gave each other dripping parting kisses.

A kitten wound itself around our legs and suddenly a figure emerged from the gray ribbons, sprang under our front roof and called: Ah, it's you, Beatrix.

God. I was startled. Herr Knoll from the third floor, who dragged a shrunken leg along. He was supposed to have had polio as a child. Behind his thick coke-bottle glasses, reptilian eyes quickly and pitilessly seized me and Kaspar, his victims, and without one further word he unlocked the door, let me and the cat through, leaving Kaspar outside. Knoll had sized up the situation, knew what game was playing itself out here, knew what was going on, running against the grain of orderliness. A last, short lizard glance at me.

That Beatrix, in this wet condition, her movements uncontrolled, with a man at the door, with no keys. That dots the i on what I have long since known about her. He hobbled hurriedly up the stairs to his floor, in the certainty that no one would ever be able to convince him of the contrary.

As I arrived upstairs at the end of our hall, a gigantic black silhouette stood in the doorframe. My brother, Uli—Paul Bunyan; behind him bits of my mother. Aha, was all I could think. I felt sick.

…were so worried!…my mother.

So where have you been!?…Uli.

God, look at you!?…Uli.

Do you know how late it is?…my mother.

With the last energy I could still muster, my legs pulled themselves together and stomped toward my room.

'Night, I said, stretching, stretching my neck above all, holding my head as if I were balancing a glass and thinking as I did so of only one thing: reconquering my dignity in this fragile present with the bearing of a queen.

The Raft

DON'T GIVE ME ANY BULLSHIT. It doesn't take much to get a girl's heart running hot, said Johnny Hubmann.

You're nuts, I said from up above. Since we had climbed out of the train that brought us into this village at the edge of the Alps, the gigantic Johnny Hubmann had been carrying me on his shoulders.

It was May, and the Hot Club of Munich was hosting the yearly rafting trip for its members. I was quite new in these illustrious circles and my expectations had been animated to a peak during the train trip. There were about eighty of us, and, as soon as we climbed aboard the train, the mood was cranked up like a merry-go-round. Seasoned party animals stood up on the benches in our car, fiddled with their beer bottles, repeated sleazy jokes they had known forever, exchanged boasts, filled with anticipation of the great gaudy that drew nearer with each chug of the train.

Someone from the Dixieland band blew on his trumpet and drove the collective excitement into orgiastic hysteria. The May alpine landscape chased past the train windows in kaleidoscopic tatters of color.

I had come alone. I had separated from Kaspar. Without a direct pretext, without a compelling reason, without a scene. A sort of thaw in our four-year relationship, caused by new interests entering our environment like a hot breeze. Little omens, a much-too-strong swat without warning when I had a bloodsucking mosquito on my arm. My explosive impatience at waiting for Kaspar, who always took his time. Transparent excuses. We were busy deconstructing our identities. When we met, we had looked about, curious, greedy for novelty; now we finally, gradually, let go of one another.

In the illustrious society aboard the train I was the new kid on the block. My credentials were carefully examined, shoved hither and thither like a souvenir, grabbed, I was asked my name and—Hey, you, move over, over there! someone said to someone. On my right a spot came free and right away a new lad garnered it for himself.

I remember this train trip with the same feeling as I do the trampling of grapes in a gigantic tub on the island of Ischia, years later. Just as then, I had made an important decision all on my own. Just as then, lusty pushing and shoving all around me, in a narrow space, paired with the melancholy feeling of what had been—giving way to wild applause for the new.

After the one-hour train trip, which seemed much longer to us because of the joyous uproar, we reached our destination. The party danced from the train through the streets of the town, toward the river. Round about us spring was bursting out everywhere. An intoxicated euphoria filled the Moränen country of the lower Alps after the long icy winter. A fresh breeze still blew from white-capped mountain peaks, but the catkins were already blooming on the willows, bees were buzzing about every source of nectar, birds shot up from their newly built nests. And wherever one stepped out of the shadows, rays of sunlight streamed from the azure blue sky. People passed tanning oil around, as many of them had already taken off their clothes and were walking towards the river in their bathing suits, in bikinis, barefoot.

The river Isar wears two hats. The first, the river as river, flat and unpredictable, curves between, jagged cliffs, gravel pits and islands, sometimes rushing, then once again seeking its sluggish way. From the nourishing mud, gargantuan willows bend out from the bank in greeting. There, roots, stripped trees, and every sort of river detritus had fled during the spring thaw.

The second Isar, the canal, flows in deep green predictability, held in check, through a concrete bed. The height differentials on the way down to the flatland are regulated by gates that simultaneously supply energy to the surrounding communities.

It smelled green and minty, the first brimstone butterflies bewitched the air, and there, behind the bridge, on the canal, the raft lay waiting for us, held to the bank with ropes. A large, flat thing made of thick tree trunks tied together. In the middle reigned a kind of wooden tart as a podium for the musicians. Next to it there was still room for seating and for a keg of beer. On a long board covered with a blue and white tablecloth, a meal awaited: pretzels, sausages, radishes, mustard and butter. The blue-and-white diamond pattern and the Bavarian lion served as flag, fluttering at the end of the raft.

I sat in my bikini on a thick tree trunk and trailed my naked legs in the water. I was full of expectation, excited and uncertain. Everything so new. The green sun caressed my body, silver flowing pleats accompanied the raft. Down on the riverbed, between watercress and algae salad, spotted trout and fat gudgeons thrashed about. We swung on past black evergreen watchmen that alternated with the filigree of birch trees in absinthe green, and fruitful meadows, pink and spotted yellow. Lupines, lilacs, and a hut in which hay was stored for the winter; and further along, a pair of bicyclists. Startled upward by the shrill cry of the clarinets, a raven fled a few branches further up. All around me they were dancing to Dixieland music, as if they were struggling for oxygen. Drank great quantities on top of it, Bavarian beer from a barrel. Brewed in spring after Lent, it had the highest alcohol content. And whoever felt sweat running down his body simply jumped into the ice-cold water.

Amidst this lusty tumult, which bound us all up paradisaically with the rhapsody of the water and the joyous dust-up of the music, I felt an excitement that absorbed me completely, the ecstatic moment before a leap. And the man with the pipe dived and surfaced here and there amid the illustrious company. I knew he was our host, the entrepreneur behind the Hot Club.

The picture before us fleshed itself out. Two fishermen with a hunting dog stood on the bank of the canal. The raft moved cozily toward them. Everyone was agape. In the curiosity about the unexpected lurked an event. The two fishermen held their hands in front of their foreheads, to block the light, gazing

expectantly. The dog first ran toward us along the bank of the canal, then alongside the raft, raging, snapping at us.

Whistling and yodeling and laughing across, and the anglers back at us.

You've got some cute fillies there, called one of them, whistling through his
fingers.

In that instant I found myself lifted high over the heads of my fellow travelers.
You mean her?

This one? the voice below me repeated.

Yeah, her, and that one over there.

Raucous screaming in every direction. Then I felt the wooden planks beneath
my feet again.

A hand still held me firmly. I turned to encounter a mouth hot with sun.

We both laughed, loudly, embarrassed.

Our meeting was unavoidable, come, sit down with me, he said and popped his pipe back into his mouth.

The hand with the blue ring led mine. I went along behind him. In the corner of my eye, little clouds of pipe smoke swirled past me, dissolved in the colored haze of the meadows, the dark cover of the evergreens; but for now I was looking only at him. Dissecting him with the jubilant ecstasy of an ornithologist on whom it dawns that he is holding in his hand a species entirely new to him. We found a place at a distance from the uproar. I took his hand and studied the ring, which was already more familiar than the man himself.

So where did you get that lovely ring? I asked.

Do you know the film *Jud Süss*? A masterpiece of propaganda from the Hitler era.

I shook my head.

Ferdinand Marian gave it to me. He played Jud Süss.

I nodded but did not trust myself to ask any more questions, since I had no idea what he was talking about.

The brown of Ferdinand's suntanned chest, his arm, tobacco smoke, musk from his perspiration enwrapped me, or rather, enwrapped what was still left of my familiar self. My strength, which just minutes before had held me up solidly like the inseparable cartilage of the spine, fled like a thief. Dixieland music roared out past us. Trumpets peppered the startled landscape with buckshot. The drums made the raft shake, and the tones of the clarinet flew around the rhythm with the elegance of a swallow. In my throat sat the listener's knot.

So how old are you? Ferdinand asked.

Eighteen.

Wow, so young, he said, laughing loudly.

CaryGrantRhettButler, the man I had just met, who was sitting so close to me, immediately wove me into his tales.

I want to celebrate my divorce with you, he said earnestly.

And I acted as if that were the most natural thing in the world. I wanted to appear sophisticated.

He continued: The countess ripped me off. Impoverished aristo, you know...I rescued her when she was pregnant, penniless, I married her practically off the street and never breathed a word about Puppi not being my daughter. I gave her my name. I set the countess up in a shop, spirits and tobacco, she managed to pry that loose as well.

Here and there he drew on his pipe, blew it clean, fetched a small folded instrument from his cavernous trouser pocket, took his arm off my shoulder to scratch the pipe clean. Tap it clear on one of the logs. The packet of tobacco was already lying ready on his knee. He held a pinch between thumb and forefinger.

Smell, he said. Dunhill. From London. Very fine.

I sniffed—tobacco and figs—and gave a thrilled nod. His hand formed a shelter around the pipe bowl, and he sucked in the flame. Little smoke signals steamed out. His warm arm lay once again around my shoulder. Naked bodies, beer and Dixieland, water, raft were all out there; in here, us, a four-leaf clover, in entranced wonder.

The countess totally exploited and two-timed me. She didn't tell me she was expecting a gigantic settlement. She was a Pückler. Prince Pückler. Get it? A gigantic sum, 500,000DM. What she did behind my back...hired a lawyer, started sleeping with him, all behind my back...

In my throat the listener's knot.

Sluice! Ladies to higher ground! a voice cried out.

We felt how the water drew us with it, faster and faster, towards a bridge where the canal abruptly broke off. Shrieking and laughter, our belongings above our heads, we raced toward the cliff edge. The raft, all of us, delivered over to fate, shot down the water rail and dunked into a swirling whirlpool as we reached the bottom.

For a moment we stood up to our knees in the water, until the raft bobbed up again. Forgotten utensils, shoes, pieces of clothing, cigarette boxes danced along behind us, until they were full and drunk and sank into the river grass.

Relieved after surviving the danger, drinking our beer again, dancing and raging to the Dixieland music peppering its perfect shrill rhythm into the landscape. I too danced amidst this lustily organized paradise of a nonconforming form, to which I too now belonged.

The swift reordering after the wet chaos was directed by Ferdinand using his pipe as baton. He took his place near the band on the podium, as our host in the mobile raft inn. Through the finely ground rings in my gigantic beer mug, I saw an interrupted Ferdinand, much higher above me, in the parrot green of the trees, the snapshot of a blackbird, its beak full of dragonfly. A grinning face thrust itself forward, broke up in phosphor and said: Cheers!

Ferdinand bellowed, his bare feet, his trouser cuffs rolled up, right next to me.

Listen up! Pipe down! All right, ladies and gentlemen. We have sailed through Scylla and Charybdis superbly. Now for the next leg of our odyssey. The dangerous Sirens still lie before us. It will be announced. Plug your ears.

Loud drum roll.

I have here a sweet little siren, and I am going to have her sing me something. With that he left the podium and held me close.

Sheer thunder from the drums, trumpet blasts.

Trixi! Trixi! the crowd shrieked and exulted round about me. I felt myself lifted up by something monstrous, and tried in this hovering state to keep my reserves under my command even as they melted away. But a quick succession of small explosions in my nervous system opposed the regime of order.

In the course of the day we wound our way through the landscape at the speed determined for us by our supplies and energy, gliding with every meter further down into the flatland. The fine nuances of the flora and fauna unfolded before our eyes. The shade trees reached further to the sky, their branches stretching in paradisaically lusty submission, leaves magnifying themselves as if by magic. Swarms of birds whirled everywhere. The surrounding meadows and fields intensified their luxurious offering as we galloped our way down.

The primal recipe of fertility, transience and resurrection, Kandinsky's bouquet; the colors of the blossoms shrieked, saccharin scent everywhere, an offering of a billion bees, bugs in shimmering plastic armored tanks, and, to top it off, the breathtaking couture of butterflies.

Late afternoon. The raft and we ourselves cast dark silhouettes along the riverbank. The sun lapped at the farms, the bulbous spires, the fruit gardens. Bicycle riders traveled with their shadows. Cars rolled down their windows to wave at us, drove a short ways next to us, until the street veered them off with it: the unpredictability of fate.

From the awakening nucleus of my young life, without the least trace of sentimentality, this journey points its infallible, omnipotent finger at the objective interwovenness of time and place.

As the evening sun ducked below the horizon, the sky above us turquoise, in the east the intimation of night, we landed at the raft dock. With firm ground beneath our feet once again, exhausted by the loud music and beer, the beer above all, a few people gave up the necessity of making sense and fumbled their way to the tram station under the protection of comrades. We were a tired caravan. New friends held one another by the hand, to keep the magnetic field together as long as possible. Beside the path lay remains of an old raft, rotting away. Between its trunks, daisies had bored their way through, in a symmetric pattern. A yelping cur ran alongside. Through the trees pressed color dabs of tents, a snake of smoke curled up and steamed away. It smelled of schnitzel.

Exhausted and excited, Ferdinand and I sauntered along the soft path beneath the leafy umbrella, his arm around my shoulder. Next to me a third person hopped along: my heart, irrepressible as a child. I had been inducted into the dance of the Bohemians, they called me a doll, hot chick, touching their forefingers to their tongues as if they had burned themselves.

Those who were still not tired, their heads turned by the beer, sang loudly, as if there were a contest to win:

Der Mensch hat einen Kopf,	*Man has a head,*
Der Kopf reicht ihm nicht aus,	*The head does not suffice him,*
Versuch es nur mit Deinem Kopf,	*Try living just with your head,*
Lebt höchstens eine Laus	*It might work for a louse at best*
Denn für dieses Leben	*For when it comes to this life*
Ist der Mensch nicht klug genug	*Mankind is just not clever enough*

The people waiting at the tram stop jostled close together and gave mistrustful glances from the corner of their eyes at the loud, colorful, band of vagabonds drawing near.

Amber evening sun got caught in the window glass of the approaching tram, violet tassels in the scaly sky waved the day farewell.

Love

I PACKED MY PAINTING TOOLS into a doctor's bag, my prettiest clothes and my jeans, an apron to muck up, shoes, books.

Take your raincoat along, it always rains in Salzburg, my mother called out from the living room.

I packed almost everything I owned, as I was going away for six weeks, six whole weeks, to study with Oskar Kokoschka in summer session.

I had never been away from my parents for so long. Only at the weekends, the fabricated weekends, when, with my skis and with my rucksack packed full, as if I were traveling to see my girlfriend Uschi in the mountains, I would climb off the tram three stops later and drop everything in Kaspar's room.

Months before, I had seen the notice on a placard at the Academy in Munich and immediately registered in Salzburg. The course was called *The School of Seeing* and cost quite a bit. But through my work as a model I was always able to earn money and did not need to ask anything of anyone.

As the anticipation of my journey mounted, I passed the time impatiently with my fellow students in my anatomy class. My attention wandered from my sheet of drawing paper, where a skinless charcoal arm displayed red and blue veins, which were to enliven the biceps, and beyond it, the cartilage of the elbow. The professor stood before me as if in a fog. Next to him, on a metal table with casters, lay the solitary torso, missing the rest of its extremities, revolting in its gray whiteness.

Certainly I heard the professor explaining the lamentable object in every detail. But in my head it melted away into a muscular brown arm and, without my willing it, Ferdinand stood before me in the flesh. With the blue and red pencils in my hand, I stared over the heads in front of me at the figure of the professor, who tapped about with his stick between the torso on the table and us students, moving his mouth like a robot.

I heard none of what he said. I had jazz playing in my ear.

I ducked beneath a little door and walked toward the music into the gloomy vault, above which lay the Augustiner Biergarten. It smelled of old money, cool and musty. Further, deeper within, in dim light stood a table. A candle on it, next to a bar, on which a few girls were sitting with beer bottles in their hands, idly swinging their legs. A piece of music streamed from the adjoining vault.

> *They said you have a blue guitar*
> *You do not play things as they are*
>
> *Tschu, Tschu, Tschu… The man replied:*
> *Things as they are, are changed upon the blue guitar*

I had landed in the Augustiner basement, beneath the earth, in the legendary Hot Club. And there, at a table, stood Ferdinand, waiting, glass in hand. He daubed the red entry stamp in the warm crook of my arm, took his pipe out of his mouth and pressed me to him, drew me in with the vehemence of a player at the roulette table, drew me on into the tunnel room, where the music billowed.

Above the dancing couples trembled a cloud of cigarette smoke. Hot-red faces turned toward the candlelight. In the twilight on the walls, as if in an archaic dream, cave drawings, scribblings, ancient longings, magic symbols etched in stone. Rows of benches and tables lost themselves in the darkness of the extensive vault.

A ring formed just below the stage; in the midst of it Veruschka, soon to be the most famous of models, stamped her foot to the music like a Maasai warrior. A couple of black men lounged idly near the stage, cigarettes between their lips at odd angles. We were fascinated by these exotic creatures from America. We admired them. Wet light caught on honey skin, they wore shrill bow ties with pink shirts, brown suits with razor creases. Here they hung tightly together and one could feel how they were not altogether certain about this total admiration streaming from the uniformly fair-skinned group of people dancing to their music.

Here everything was the same for everyone, even the toilets. No signs saying *no colored, whites only*. Not just that but waves of applause into the bargain. To us they appeared infinitely cool. We studied them, the palms of their hands lighter than their other skin, their white laughter.

That's Louis Armstrong after his concert in the Kongresshalle, that's really him, whispered Ferdinand and gestured toward the indolent group.

A member of the Isar-Chicks-Dixie-Band handed Satchmo his trumpet, and no one was dancing any more. We all gaped breathlessly at him.

Notes shot and bubbled from the golden instrument, were caught by the vault and descended in a pulsating shower of sound drops. Notes flew around the room as light as birds. Much too narrow a cage. The music bumped against the moist walls, slithered out through smallest openings.

Satchmo set his trumpet aside, his singing raw and rasping, as if his wind-pipe were falling apart. Black genius right here among us.

Oh, the shark has pretty teeth, dear
And he shows them, pearly white
Just a jackknife has Macheath, dear
And he keeps it out of sight

When the shark bites
With his teeth, dear
Scarlet billows start to spread
Fancy gloves though wears Macheath, dear
So there's not a trace of red
Oh, yeah.

We raged, shrieked and stamped our feet, were beside ourselves, beside ourselves with excitement in the cloudburst of applause.

•

The car smelled of dog and copper pennies. Adi drove, Fritz sat next to her, with me in the back between my piles of luggage, beside me Father's dog Lexi. Our route led down the autobahn, through the landscape rooms of my childhood. The grandiose necklace of the alpine giants ran alongside us: steep, jagged cliffs, monstrosities losing themselves southward in delicate pink. I could think of only one thing: ending the journey as soon as possible, arriving in Salzburg. But the further we got from Munich the more my father's interest in the landscape awakened: suddenly he gave a start and peered curiously through the window like an animal scenting a trail.

Come on, Adi, take the exit! Let's cruise in on the road to Berchtesgaden and have lunch at Angermeier's.

My mother, jolly: Yes, that is what we shall do.

Her beautiful face smiled at me in the rear-view mirror. Next to it, mirrored, my carefully painted fire-red Revlon mouth. Once we had turned off the autobahn, Lexi yelped at every cow grazing along the fence, the imaginary enemy she would like to bite dead through the car window. Unmoved by the racket to his rear, my father lost himself in reflections. As often happened, it was from a mixture of homesickness and scientific interest, in farm life above all. He rolled down his window. Word tatters flew back to me and eloped with my dreamy absence.

Adi, drive slowly. That's Castle Reichertsbäuern over there. Perhaps we will see it.

My mother, curious, stuck out her neck in the direction my father indicated. I felt ill from sitting in the back seat and from an uncontrollable fear that took ever greater control of me: that we would never arrive, that I would never again see Ferdinand, that his promise to visit me in Salzburg would vanish into the obscure distance of separation. Indescribable panic crept up within me, as if I were standing at the furthest edge of a cliff that, through the car window, at no great distance, seemed close enough to grasp.

In Salzburg we will celebrate it all, Ferdinand had whispered to me when we last saw one another. Everything. My divorce and my birthday.

Here in the car, I found myself at an impassible chasm of my imagination. My parents were using this journey as a reason for a junket in the lower Alps, instead of bringing me to Salzburg with all possible speed and leaving me there by myself so that I could pull myself together, begin my studies with the great Oskar Kokoschka, and at the same time abandon myself to sleepless nights full of anxiety (for in my heart sat the fear that Ferdinand would not come to Salzburg) andfull of excitement (at the possibility of a visit, as announced by Ferdinand).

Look over there, the farm with the brewery. I could have bought that for next to nothing back then.

Tja, Fritzl, but those were hard times.

They had forgotten me completely in my back-seat nest, forgotten our destination. They had spun themselves all the way into their usual rudimentary view of missed opportunities, entangling themselves—particularly the pessimist Fritz—in senseless labyrinths of memory.

When we finally arrived at the Angermeier Inn, Adi reached Fritz his cane and her arm. Stiff from sitting in the car, they moved like snails toward the beer garden, and beneath one of the trees searched with all possible ado for an appropriate table. My nerves, stretched to bursting, were pulling on filigree threads while my father read loudly from the menu, smacking his lips with gusto, imagining the various dishes.

My mother cheerily agreed, praised the setting of the *établissement*, the mild day, the birds above us in the branches, the well-behaved dog Lexi, the waitress grasping four bier steins in each hand, the distinguished-looking married couple at the next table, the odor of food around us, the flower arrangements on the tables.

Alongside all the idyllic considerations and the time my parents were frittering away, the unavoidable thought of The Letter was sneaking up on me.

I had written Ferdinand a letter that now felt like a stroke of idiotic genius. I had used the occasion of my temporary absence from Munich to make a gushing revelation of my love. And now, on account of this one-sided confession, I yearned for his answer. At the same time I had never before been so plagued by doubt as by the uncertainty of its arrival. I had written in a fit of narcissism. Now I regretted not first having waited for a letter from him, if one would have arrived at all.

In this condition of complete vulnerability, I was skeptically sentimental, at the mercy of my sensitive modesty.

•

In Salzburg I lived in a little room in the house of a carpenter's family. The singing stairs that led to the first floor played the traitor. One could not come or go without their loudly announcing it. The carpenter's informant-wife was always standing there at the open kitchen door, her arms crossed into a corset supporting her bosom. She cast her cold gaze upon me in the cool corridor, in whose odious silence my shoes loudly clattered.

Y'all r up mighty early today. Y'all in a hurry? Got some coffee, nice 'n fresh.

My simple, suspicious lodging seemed designed for espionage. The front door cawed, the courtyard gate bleated, until I finally found my way out onto the street.

I scurried across the bridge over the River Salzach, through the freshly washed narrow cobblestone streets of the old town, further along to the mountain tram station that brought me to the citadel. Up above, in the castle courtyard, a few chickens were scratching about in the sand in front of a medieval porter's lodge. Red geraniums were hanging from the window boxes. At a short distance, under a chestnut tree, waited a group of young people who turned their heads to follow me, I imagined; I was so excited that I felt as if I were walking in slow motion, as my inner eye watched myself moving towards them.

Is this the *School of Seeing*? I asked, my heart pounding with excitement.

Yes, we're waiting too. They nodded.

I joined the little group. After a while we were sent up ancient stone stairs trodden crooked, into a wide room with a cruciform vaulted ceiling.

At one end of the room the windows looked down into a toy world, the red tile rooves of Salzburg. Arterial boulevards pushed through the green treetops, full of cars that crept onward like beetles. In the distance the land stretched all the way to the mountains, surrounding playful miniature red and white houses, in sporadic groups, with bulbous spires in their midst. At the other end of the medieval knightly hall yawned a gigantic open fireplace. Here Oskar Kokoschka held his lessons, his *School of Seeing*.

First his assistant introduced himself: Kortukrax, whose name interwove itself with the Latin word *appropinquare* into the inmost sanctum of my earlier memories. Likewise Kortukrax's outward appearance: stocky form, broad shoulders, the head on guard, leaning slightly forward, bushy dark hair matched with an unkempt bushy beard. Always a cigarette in the corner of the mouth, or between the index and middle fingers, which were yellowish-brown from smoking. Bare remnants of brown teeth through which he moistly spoke. He always wore black: a solemn, elegant vest, with white open shirt collar. Thus he had styled his exterior with the utmost care.

We each got an easel, grouped ourselves in a ring around a podium on which a nude woman let her flowered robe glide from her shoulder. We were to do a speed watercolor, as she was moving in slow motion, a method that schools the eye. We had to learn firmly to hold on to everything essential, with the greatest concentration. We worked according to Kortukrax's instructions, and the weighty way he prepared us for the master had us feverishly awaiting the entrance of the great genius, as patients await the doctor. And then finally, one afternoon…swift feet up the stairs.

Pssst, pssst, silence. Professor Kokoschka. If he stops next to one of you, leaf through your work and listen to what he has to say, said Kortukrax in a stage whisper.

And before us stood Kokoschka, tall and slender, an elderly gentleman. He stopped to catch his breath. Gray hair, short, clinging to his perfectly oval head. Self-assured and warm, his smiling greetings radiated curiosity across our little circle, the robust reality of his appearance turning our stupid fear into an old ghost.

Everything you see standing around you is mirrored in the model's body. That's not just beige or pink. No. That contains every color. Light, shadow, the clothes you're wearing. It has to sum it all up. Every color is pregnant with its environment. Thus Master Kokoschka instructed us in Austrian dialect.

We quickly discovered how vain he was. We traveled to Vienna, where O.K. was opening a great exhibition of his works. As we students thronged about him on the terrace of the museum, he threw open its doors, calling out: Voila, you now behold the art of the century.

He thought nothing of Picasso, did not think much of any of his contemporaries. We, his pupils, we waited, waited in vain for praise that could hint the way into our future. But except for a friendly pat on the shoulder—yes, yes, that's quite nice…no, that won't work—we remained stuck in our own misty dreams.

I remember it as a splendid period. I made friends with the others. Together with pupils of Giaccomo Manzu, who headed the sculpture class and had done a bust of me, we drank new Heuriger wine in the evenings and talked shop, our eyes closed to the reality beyond our consciousness. We discovered new realities and new happiness, our hearts full of dubious youthful wisdom. *Really everything out there is crap.*

An important event burst into the warm summery days up on the mountain. A photographer and a journalist from *Quick* magazine traveled in from Munich to photograph me with O.K. Me? Yes. They wanted to report on me and my work with the master. Suddenly I was at the centre of my social circle.

I was accustomed enough to standing in front of cameras, but I remember my shyness, bordering on fainting, at being pushed forward this way. I had great respect for Kokoschka and felt privileged, well aware that a genius was tutoring us. Being vain, he thought the magazine story wonderful and helped me get past my shyness, put his arm around me and enjoyed it.

A sort of student-master bond with O.K. developed after the photo episode. He tarried a little longer at my easel, I leafed through my aquarelles:

You already showed me that one, he said.

I invited him sometimes to join our little troop of friends in our favorite pub. We would sing songs for him. He took pleasure in our youth, our fresh cheeks, our relaxed laughter, listened to our as-yet-unlived philosophies, which he acknowledged with smiling nods. We gave him little kisses, smooches, as he called them, which he tucked away like gems, along with our teasing and nakedly flirtatious remarks.

Only when we met him on the street with his English wife, who trudged primly along next to him like a governess, did he act indifferent. He looked over at us, at me, only fleetingly, or not at all. He walked past us on the arm of his strait-laced wife, every bit the dignified professor. We giggled, played along by politely greeting them.

The *Quick* with the article was published. I was the cover girl, still too young and clueless—spoiled, too, in those days—to grasp what is called cosmic synchronicity, to see it as a building block in a career. Everything I encountered was exciting, had the same value.

I am holding in my hand a letter in which a Munich businessman who made a postwar fortune in scrap metal, a Mr. Bierlein, offers to buy all my Salzburg watercolors when I bring them home at the end of my studies with Oskar Kokoschka. He names an exuberant price.

And then finally, one day, as I slipped in through the treasonously creaking gate, the carpenter's wife came towards me with a weighty mien.

I got somethin fa you.

And in the kitchen, with her thumb and forefinger, she plucked a letter from the picture frame that enclosed Saint Lazarus.

You done got a letter from Mr. Ferdinand Anton from Munich, a big fat one.

I let myself drop into a chair right there by the mailwoman, felt nothing of the moist tabletop, nothing of the mulch pile of razor-thin rhubarb husks next to it, smelled nothing of the cooking scent that suffused the kitchen as incense the nave.

A letter from Ferdinand. My letter had encouraged him. He felt the same tenderness—he dreamed of me day and night—a fairy from another world—a new, never suspected perspective—new faith in his future, after having been cornered by the phantoms of doubt...

A short while later I sat down on a bench beneath a linden tree in front of the train station and awaited the arrival of a train from Munich. A young blond buck did one circuit around my island, parked his bike and flopped down next to me. He gave me a fresh little grin; on his fleshy nose blackheads sat like fly droppings. He pompously lit a cigarette in his cupped hands and puffed across to me as a conversational thread.

A cock pigeon tottered around a pigeon lady, to the accompaniment of the sensuous rhyme from his puffed-up throat. The church tower rang the hour. Above the heads of the people waiting in the station building flitted swallows. A porter daubed the pearls of sweat from his forehead with a red-and-white handkerchief. Behind him, a buxom citizen in a Salzburg Loden outfit, Austrian clogs, impatiently directed her chauffeured Mercedes and the carrier with his cart toward what she judged to be the simplest access to the on-ramp.

A train whistle trilled across the general noise, evoking my own shrill inner tumult. My hair-trigger nerves and an off-putting insecurity tore at me, danced in synch with my feelings, and, at the same time, discordantly against them; I perceived every triviality, particles of reality and illusion alike.

I looked nervously at the clock, felt about for the suitcase next to my legs, under the bench. The silver bell of the bicycle at the tree stole a rust-red glow from the sharp ray of sunlight shooting forth from beneath a family of clouds. I slipped onto the edge of my waiting-room bench, to keep a sharp eye on the squads of people that streamed in and out of the dimly lit station like breakers. At the edge of the bench I lurked, lying in wait for the wondrous day after tomorrow.

Ferdinand saw me there under the tree right away. His bouquet of roses fanned out like a flame above the heads of the hurriedly streaming masses.

I sprang up onto the bench.

Fer-di-naand! Feeer-dii-naaand! I cried with delight.

The 'i' flew like a tiny emissary. Tingaling, tingaling, a tram squeaked as it wedged its way in between us, so loudly that it burst one's eardrums.

•

In the hotel, which we reached on foot from the station, the porter stared strictly above his glasses frames, my passport in his hand. Ferdinand maneuvered a bill across the ratty counter. The porter grinned and shoved the exonerating document back the same way, tapping his peaked cap understandingly.

In the upstairs hall the room numbers were stamped into the wooden centers of the doors, like branding on the rear of a cow, and on one of the doors stood printed in black-and-white enamel: WC.

My heart dense with underbrush. I wasn't so sure about this...

Ferdinand opened the door. The worn-down key went *kraaaach*. We gave an embarrassed laugh and stumbled across a step down into the little room.

I can see the room before me, the slender bed, only half of which was visible, the half with the pillows. The foot of the bed vanished through an opening in the wall and made room up above for an underwear drawer. Next to it wedged a tiny table, next to an even tinier sink, tight by the window. I leaned out. Down below there slumped a coal hut, suffocated by the summery snow of an elderberry bush. Then the view bumped into windowless gray, opposite.

Only one person could sit on the amputated bed. We had as yet no practice unburdening our hearts with words. With the expert's finesse Ferdinand's hand peeled my skittish body from its hull of clothing, which proceeded to embrace his shirt and trousers down on the floor. We up above fell upon one another wordlessly. It was the only possibility.

Later I walked with Ferdinand to a pub and introduced him to my friends. We drank insane quantities of new Heuriger wine. On the way back to our love coffin, the moon hung in the sky in the center of a wide white vapor ring, like a fried egg.

We ran along, holding our heads majestically high. I had to be careful not to jumble up the arrangement of words in my head. Zither music and laughter tempted one from the open windows of inns. Above us, in the branches of a tree, a kitten meowed, and Ferdinand insisted on rescuing it. Dazzled by the wine, he clambered up the branch with the luck of a sleepwalker, popped the little cat into his jacket pocket. During his breakneck descent he sang loudly, with jarring tones. I laughed, completely debilitated by the first attack wave of love.

Ferdinand whispered into my hair, tattooed my heart with a sandstorm of grandiose promises, and I believed every word.

I lay awake for a long time in the narrowness of the sleeping-cave. At irregular intervals the tram glided across the ceiling, the imprint of a beast danced across the blanket, across Ferdinand's arm. At that point I must have dreamed off. *Immorality and Chaos*, in big red letters, ran through my dream like an endless loop—*Immorality and Chaos*, above the doorway of an all-you-can-eat restaurant.

In the morning I told Ferdinand the dream, and he laughed and laughed and pressed me into the shabby hotel pillow, upon which the early sun emerged in triumph from some indiscernible source, pinkish red, in silent brilliance.

The Mother

MY FATHER LOVED THE SIMPLE PEOPLE, "little people with no shadows, whose feet leave no prints."

Way off base, he always said. They are the salt of every nation. He was fascinated by the way they accepted their fate, accommodated themselves to the inevitable. He listened silently, nodded or adopted a skeptical mien when someone came to him with dubious stories. Back then on our estate, Father was the embodiment of justice. But whenever the opportunity presented itself, when one of our workers made himself conspicuous at the office door, which was always open, Fritz encouraged the shy complainant

Do come in, Niedermayer, what's the matter?

Whereupon he was fully engaged, whether it was a question of a quarrel, or a financial emergency, or an illness.

We sat around the table having coffee and cake. My mother pushed a plate with an extra-large piece across to Erika. Erika's hand gestured no, she shook her head. No, she did not want anything.

Coffee?

No, thanks very much, she said decidedly.

She did not want anything. No cake crumbs falling down, hanging in the corner of one's mouth. No slurping hot coffee. No, thanks.

With the elegance and audacity of youth I had introduced Ferdinand to my parents as my grand amour, the love of my life. And now we had brought Erika, Ferdinand's mother, home with us.

Everyone looked at her attentively. My father, my mother, I and Ferdinand. I sat expectantly. The scenes Anita's "inappropriate" marriage had caused were still vivid in my memory, and I wanted to put the introduction of Mother Erika behind me as quickly as possible. I was in league with Ferdinand. My parents' ideas were an obstacle, true, but I would overcome anything. Love of Ferdinand had transformed me into a beast.

Ferdinand beamed contentedly. Him I had already brought home a few times. My father called Ferdinand the "day milker" and did not take him very seriously. He thought about how young I still was; also, he thought about my otherwise "cool" judgment, which he could always trust.

Beatrix is no fool. She really knows how to think things through. Doesn't let anyone put anything over on her.

Ferdinand's visits to my parents were something of a surprise attack: presenting himself as if on stage, he could turn on his great charm like fireworks. One stared in astonishment from one episode to the next. He made my father laugh, and laughed right along with him, as if he were hearing his own anecdotes for the first time. All the while he busied himself with his pipe ritual. Scratch it out, blow it clean, refill it, pack it close, light it. Fascinating.

My father bent sociably across the table to Erika.

Do tell us then, Mother Erika, how'd you come to Munich?

We sized her up expectantly.

Except for Frau Rieder, the woman who cleaned the house, who simply did her work, who came and went and never got coffee nor cake, no representatives of the "simple folk" had visited us here in the city. One could see what Erika was thinking: that she did not belong in this room. Warily hanging her head a little forward, leaning it to the side, full of mistrust, stretching her dressy apron with its flower pattern, she balanced her heavy, squat body like a weight on the edge of the chair, as if she would be leaping up and running off any moment. With her right hand she held her purse on her knees, firmly embracing it. The left hand snapped the catch open, shut, open, shut.

In her broad, soft face, helpless astonishment stood like a question mark.

She fixed on my father with the unsteady gaze of an anxious bird. It was to him alone, Fritz Ost, that she wished to tell her story. Him, as an authority figure.

I come from Lower Bavaria, she began…

There were eleven children at home. It was cramped. Four in a bed.

When she turned sixteen she climbed on the train to Munich, to find work there. It was the next sister's turn to take care of the younger siblings. One mouth less to feed, quite simply.   My father nodded.

Yes, so it always was, and so it still is.

Yeah, 'n then I jes' went from door te door, til I gotta job.

The competent Erika was soon awarded the post of house manager in an apartment building adjoining the English Garden.

They done tore it down then, when that Hitler done widened the roads. Ferdinand was born there.

She had met her husband, Ferdinand's father, when she sat down one day on a bench to catch her breath, while carrying a load of laundry. He asked where she worked, how much she earned, then whether she would like to meet up with him again.

Yes, she thought so, since he looked dashing. He was a bricklayer. But now he was not good for much of anything and she couldn't bring him along, nowhere.

He ain't got nothin' to say, and he drinks too much.

We listened in silence. She went on to tell us about the professor who lived on the third floor. He had stroked her boy's head, patted his cheek, said as he went past, hey, how goes it, young man? It was not surprising, since Ferdinand was a spectacularly pretty child, headful of dark locks, brown skin, blue eyes.

So what are you doing? said the child, looking up from the landing.

I'm going to my students.

What's that you have in your briefcase?

Notebooks I have to correct...So what do you want to be when you grow up?

A tram conductor.

I see, I see.

Over the years they had developed a stairwell friendship, the pretty boy and the professor.

The professor said to Erika: such a clever little fellow, what a shame if the boy were not to attend high school.

Perhaps the professor took pity on Ferdinand. Childless himself, he felt something like paternal affection. Over the years he saw himself as a relative to the child that was always hanging around, waiting in the stairwell. Waiting for education, thought the professor. And so it happened that Ferdinand became the first link in a long chain of generations in whom this man instilled the love of learning.

Then the Professor really did send my Ferdinand to high school, said Erika proudly, smoothing her smooth apron.

Later, when I knew even more stories, and knew much more about Ferdinand's family, it struck me that the professor must inevitably have known Ferdinand's father. Perhaps the professor had come to a stop outside the building entrance, when he saw the father tottering along the street, heavy with alcohol, his legs disobedient, confused, keeping a lookout for something resembling home. A smile flitted across his elegant grownup face, so similar to his son's, when he recognized the door that marked the end of his expedition. The Professor held the door for him, stood aside to let him pass, when he saw the father rummaging at length in his pockets for the key.

Real sorry, said Ferdinand's father.

His blue eyes sparkled beneath the broad black brows. Krrrr…crept, strained, across his full mouth. He was not too tall, but he was certainly a tough cookie. One felt him exuding something dangerous. Despite his handsome face, one would not put it past him to do something sudden, brutal: a punch in the jaw, a kick in the pit of the stomach.

Mother Crabapple on her chair, crookedly. She bubbled forth as if she had to let out everything, everything. She had lapsed into a flood of talk. Memory had overtaken the present. My father had bewitched her with the art of the listener. Now there was no holding her back. She had advised her son not to marry such a young thing, in a second marriage no less, after the first one with the aristocrat had gone south. She shook her head contemptuously.

Better somethin solid, an older woman, she said.

That Johanna, *that* was the right one. Johanna, who lived in England.

Ferdinand pressed my hand under the table. This statement of Erika's stood there in the room, hardened against us in the fullness of its brutality. I smiled, looked over to my mother; steep, critical wrinkles had etched themselves onto her brow. She peered patronizingly at this woman, who had taken on way too much.

Shameless, murmured Adi.

My father saw the situation from quite a different angle. He laid his hand on Erika's shoulder. Yes, yes, there it was again—this shocking openness, cruelly direct and for that reason magical in its clarity. A small, amused smile played across his face. As it did, he nodded in agreement, as if to himself. He had to deal gingerly with the fragility of his hopes. Oh, yes, that clever Beatrix…

Young and beautiful, said my future husband, and sucked on his pipe.

An old one eats just as much, he impudently added, smiling at me. I smiled back. We were accomplices, and nothing, no one, could shatter that.

Mother Erika's bold position had spread the virus of impudence, and, to put an end to this monstrosity, Adi said to Ferdinand, her face irritable, bitter and strict:

Hopefully you will get your act together. One's daily egg is not enough.

My mother gazed out above everyone's head. She pressed her lips together so that not another word could slip out. The room grew narrower, much too narrow for the viewpoints that were colliding here. Everyone was keeping to his own place.

The simple openness that was Erika slipped down from her chair, as a sign that she now wished to end her visit. Something had gone wrong, she felt it, but like an eccentric who puts others in the wrong, she refused to accept it.

Goodbye, and many thanks, she said to the cups, the cake remnants, and stomped decidedly to the door.

Once Ferdinand and Mother Erika had gone, my father stared out the window. The powerful, straight nose, the half-pout of lip beneath his mustache, betrayed his sense of humor. The other half was hidden in shadow, like the part of his being one did not know. He laughed briefly out into the trees of the park, and looked, and looked. Then he slowly turned back toward us.

Ferdinand? He has charm, lots of nonsense in his head.

The mother is worth her weight in gold.

I had already tossed on my coat to walk to the Academy, walk away from my mother's vague remarks, from my father's weakness. It had now become simple. He was an invalid. The parents withdrew into the background, their opinion now a mere shadow. Ferdinand and I felt strong. We had conquered them, even if we had not convinced them of our reality.

Later, when I got home, it was twilight in the apartment. Not until she heard the noises that accompanied my presence did my mother click on the lamp they had both been sitting next to, reading.

Ah, I wasn't taking anything in, she said, as if by way of apology, as if I were her light. I felt guilty it was this way. My love of Ferdinand had become a brutal weapon, above all because in the family there was no talk of love. Also in the mornings I was nauseated and dizzy. We did not have much time left until we would need no more words and everyone could see it.

Proper Lies

DURING THE TIME when lovers are getting to know one another, they crave an agreement against the world out there. As a twosome, they move into another world that is like an apartment with a door they close when both have walked through, to let no one in. Thus, even at this early stage of agreement, or while craving for it, they allow no thought of doubt to arise, so that they will not be alone again—loneliness they have had enough of. The time before couplehood is no longer all that easy to visualize clearly, or they remember it as particularly lonely, now that the comparison is there to be drawn.

During the time when we were getting to know one another, and told one another everything so that we could get to know one another, during the time in which we placed each other in the harshest light, with no witnesses, believed each other's every word, because we wished to, firmly and uncritically believed in the indestructibility of love—during this time, we never entertained the thought that Love is a moody god, unpredictable, powerful like the weather. A god who, at times, rules over life and death.

So it was that, during this time, Ferdinand told me the story that began when he was fourteen, in 1943. The same age as I was in Kaspar's bed.

A sultry summer afternoon. As so often Ferdinand was delivering a pile of laundry for his mother. The address led him to the actor couple Byk and Marian.

Arriving at the address, Ferdinand found the front door open, as if someone had forgotten to close it, or had just ducked around the corner, or it had been blown open by a gust of wind.

Ferdinand went through the inviting door into the house. If he had simply set down the laundry on the hall table, the next day he would have gone back to school. Instead he stood there in the entrance with the laundry and looked about him.

From the coat hanging on a hook near the door streamed the sweet scent of perfume. He bent forward to look through another half-open door. Silk pillows nestled one another on a sofa like lovebirds. A collection of pipes on the little table next to it, candles in silver candleholders. Books were arrayed all the way up the wall. Flower-print damask shaded the windows from the outside world. On chairs, on the floor, manuscripts piled up, crumpled paper, wine glasses, half-red, and bottles.

Ferdinand stood there in the hall and stared at the luxurious chaos so alien to him. He stared because here in this room dwelt the answer to so many things. The door whispered seductively as he pushed it further open. He stepped into the room. Aha. This was how it looked, the world of the people his mother slaved away for. This was how it smelled there. This was, this must be how the characters lived in the novels he had made his friends, into whose world his fatherly friend the professor had introduced him. *Only the well-padded life is the good life*—Motifs and actions, speeches, aphorisms, whole scenes—Ferdinand knew them all, even then, although he was so young, could bring them forward and quote them. But they only half fit this chaos, strange and inviting. His eyes caught on the ratty upholstery, the silk slippers. *First comes grub, then comes morality.*

Oh, it's you, with the laundry. A voice broke in, far away yet quite nearby. At first Ferdinand had heard nothing, for he was onstage, in the middle of Brecht's class struggle. Startled, he turned around.

Hah! Caught in the act. But she smiled, with curious eyes, quizzically raising her black-penciled eyebrows. She had a fetching build and sported a negligee she must have hurriedly tossed on, casually, with a sash tied about her waist, so that her full breasts showed through.

I'm Maria Byk, she said with an ironic smile: What a pretty son Frau Erika has. She ran one hand through her rust-red hair, the other holding a burning cigarette, red from her lips.

Come, bring me the laundry upstairs, I'm by myself.

The perfume from the coat on the hook accompanied the jiggling blossoms on the negligee up the stairs. Faraway thunder played about the ankles that rode the naughty red high heels. *Tak, tak, rrrritz, rrrratz,* threatened the wooden steps. The laundry was quite a weight. As he put the load down upstairs on a chest of drawers, in a room with an unmade bed, he heard the thunder distinctly, and quite near him, her anxious:

Oh, God, a thunderstorm.

At that moment a gust of wind blew the curtains into the room. Outside a gray rushing mass of rain burst down, water poured onto the windowsill. Maria tried with all her might to close the French windows against the wind, which was now striking in full rage.

Help me, she cried.

A deafening crash of thunder followed a lightning bolt that dipped the room in white. With a scream she let go of the window and threw herself upon Ferdinand; now, he could barely close it.

You can't go now, I'm scared out of my mind! Please stay, she pleaded.

She clawed herself upon him, invading his body with an intimacy he had never yet experienced. Ferdinand held her in his boy's arms for a long time, until the storm had passed and the growl of the thunder died out beyond the rooftops.

On this afternoon young Ferdinand lost his innocence, and Maria Byk, no longer young, won her last lover. He was to protect her from many more storms.

And so it was that Ferdinand simply remained in this house, that smelled so good, smelled of affluence, culture, chaos.

When one is still half a child it is not easy to put what happens in focus. The attack of hysterical fear was not an air raid, no, it was an act of Nature. Thunder and lightning, redemption after the heat, were what commanded Ferdinand's future.

And Ferdinand esteemed himself. He became his own novelistic character. He never again went home to the cramped basement apartment, to the drunkard father and the diligent mother. He never went to school again either. The Marians took him in like a son.

Ferdinand Marian had played Jud Süss in Hitler's antisemitic propaganda film; Maria Byk was a guest actress at the Munich Kammerspiele.

Maria Byk's love affair with the fourteen-year-old Ferdinand was simply passed over in silence. No one asked, least of all among the theater set. Amid the general chaos of the war there were no rules, nothing at all compulsory. A thunderbolt catapulted Ferdinand from his narrow little world and made him free as a bird.

And thus it happened. As in a murder mystery all the factors stood ready. One gear locked into the next, to bear witness to the inevitability of fate. The sultry day; the pile of laundry that had to be delivered; the two open doors; the wind, or forgetfulness; a lightning bolt followed by a crack of thunder, whose violence invited fear; a panicked actress, ripped from her afternoon slumber, afraid above all of getting old, who had already taken to drinking in the afternoon, who forgot to close the door, who had fallen asleep in the unconscious hope of a visitor, to kill the time, the accursed time, until the evening, when the aridity of being alone could offer its hand to the uproar of the gregarious theater world. Finally.

Ferdinand sat in the Marians' wide armchairs, smoked his pipe, drank alcohol, and became an adult at warp speed. He wanted to become an actor, like both his foster parents. He studied the stage roles of young lovers. With the same greed that led him to devour history books, he gobbled up everything this new reality offered, in order to catch up, supplement his knowledge, gather up everything he refused to miss out on for any reason.

There are anonymous visions, laws graven in stone, attractions held fast in legends by passionate pens. And coincidences that burst into a life like explosions, which turn a well-told lie into an absolute truth.

The young Ferdinand looked so much like the older Ferdinand Marian that they were taken for father and son. Both had dark, wavy hair, the same profile with the lightly bowed nose, they shared the full mouth, blue gaze, brown skin, same height, and hands you could not tell apart.

How it all played out he told me in bits, but the rest I can only piece together. To fill out my description I have to enlist this confused period as a midwife. Lover, protector, and son of both; a husband tired of marriage; a drunken father in his disorientation; a longing, flight from a sour proletarian milieu; the stage play on the ship of life; crazed reality amid the barbarity of wartime.

As the air raids grew life-threatening, the Marians and Ferdinand took a little house in the country near a farmer, like many other city families.

The greenhorn Ferdinand was now the provider, for there was not much to buy, things had to be dug up. He pedaled on his bicycle through the mountainous lower Alps, scrounging for anything edible. His Lederhosen pockets were stuffed with treasures from the Marians' collection, which had lost their original meaning and received another. He knocked on the farmers' doors asking whether they had anything to eat. He had something for them too, from the actor Ferdinand Marian, something quite personal from Jew Süss. The filmstar whose manly exterior and astonishing presentation of Jud Süss had placed him among the great actors—him everybody knew.

I have here a little mouse, a valuable Vienna bronze, the mouse with the little hat and cane in its tiny paw, dancing on its hind legs.

Might you have some smoked meat, potatoes, a few eggs, a chicken, begged Ferdinand. He could also offer a Persian carpet, a blue one, one meter forty by one meter. Didn't have it with him, but for an extra bottle of schnapps he could perhaps bring the carpet by.

There was a great deal of drinking in their little house, Ferdinand told me later. Maria's quarrelsome side would come out like an incurable wound. She drank only hard liquor, and he had great trouble finding the necessary quantities of alcohol. What he was not to tell me for years was that she did not drink alone. He had grown up with an alcoholic father. So the old familiar became the new everyday.

Because he looked so dashing in his tight Lederhosen, because he smiled a divine smile, he was successful with his scavenging.

The men had been deployed to the front, or had gone missing, and there were only women to do the work. So Ferdinand often whiled away several hours at a farm. He dug a hole for a fruit tree, pitchforked hay onto a hayloft. Back in the big kitchen a pig had been slaughtered, and its bristles needed to be burned off. Here he made himself useful, joked with the girls.

You'll get part of a roast to take with you if you stay a li'l while longer. A pretty girl wound bandages around the blisters on his hands, which were unused to the hard work.

You must drink a little toast with us. Apple schnapps, or last year's cherry brandy?

The farmers' wives loaded his bicycle high; they waved, he must come again. The maidens broke off their work in the field for an entranced moment, leaned on their pitchforks, to gaze after Ferdinand with dreamy expressions. Laughing, he straddled his bike.

Sure, I'll be back soon. Cheers! His dark curls danced about his head, struggling against the wind.

The lovely treasures, the antiquities, metamorphosed into useful and edible things. The farmers had drawers stuffed with objects of marvelous value. Double layers of carpets covered wooden planks. Most of them were clueless; they knew only that the "stuff" was worth more than the eggs; and both went away happy. Each had what the other wanted.

Because of the blackout orders there were no lights, no lit windows, no open doors, the whole countryside wrapped in darkness, as if it had been crossed out from the world. Only an occasional moon. When Ferdinand pedaled homewards late at night through the winding roads in the silhouetted cutout woods, with phosphorescent foxes' eyes fixed upon him, an owl with a moth in its beak like a gray angel flew across the road right in front of his handlebars, deer paused their grazing to stare at him, as if they were relatives.

Suddenly the silhouette of another bicyclist popped up from the darkness like a frightful thought. But up ahead, drawn in charcoal, as part of the nightly pantomime, he saw his refuge: the little gabled house under the oak: redemption from a bad dream.

He opened the door into the darkness and fumbled for the candle that stood right next to the entrance, on a side table.

It's me, Maria. Silence. Scarcely was the candle alight…

You fucking bastard! screamed the voice. An indefinable object flew toward him. A hot iron landed on his upper thigh.

On the table, in the candlelight, as proof of his scavenging, lay the piece of pork, the bottle of schnapps, the potatoes. But Maria did not believe him. He smelled much too good, smelled of countryside, of rolls in the hay. He smelled like another woman, she screamed.

Later he laughed as he showed me the big scar of the iron on his upper thigh. Branded by her jealousy. The insignia of the drunkard's pantheon.

Inside the little house Maria had been waiting for him. Much too long, until the day said goodbye behind the mountain peaks. The desiccated arms of fear tapped their way through the fog of alcohol. She stared at the ominous swathe of forest that came upon her with every impatient shriek of a crow; the sound of cowbells pierced its way in through the window. The beetle in the spider's web between cupboard and table screamed with the voice of a barbarian.

While the outdoors dreamed its dream, Maria waited, waited like an Inuit for the light of spring. She had drunk up everything in the house, even the spirits from the lamp.

She sat alone in the stuffed little house, whose furniture and tchotchkes seemed to strangle her. Ferdinand Marian was always on the road. He played in the comedies designed to cheer up the German people, make them forget the war, and Maria sat there forgotten. No one was writing roles for her any more. No play, no audience, only the furniture, memories, and, outside, the lower Alps. She had visions she could dampen only with alcohol: lost beauty whispered to her; in tatters of dreams Johanna walked past her window. Applause rushed through her head like a gramophone needle on a scratched record. Ferdinand, the husband, only briefly stuck his head through the crack in the door, he had long since given up using any but the most necessary of his senses when he was home.

Ferdinand Marian, too, had annihilating sorrows. Once the war was lost, *Jud Süss*, which had made him famous, now damned him: the Allies classified *Jud Süss* as one of the most effective Nazi propaganda films, and Ferdinand Marian had the monkey of the past on his back. The bookings ran dry for the beloved star.

And yet he had never been politically engaged, had just thought selfishly of his career. Even before the war Marian had played the role of the unpleasant yet elegant bounder and lady killer, and the Nazis had exploited his popularity. At first he had refused to play Jud Süss.

From Goebbels' diary: *He hesitated to play the Jew, but I assured him he would be free to make the role attractive.*

Ferdinand Marian, in his apolitical naiveté and immense vanity, did not notice how he was being used. The same was to happen to him one more time, in the 1941 film *Ohm Krüger*, where he also played the lead. The historical film told the story of the Boer War in South Africa; it portrayed England as a ruthlessly aggressive power; and yet he had played the role, like all the others, only out of his great unquenchable thirst for love. Yes, it had always been the intoxication of the applause—and the women.

And it must have been at some point during this period that he raced into a tree. Drunk as well. The tragic thing was that the American officer in charge of film in Munich had just erased his name from the blacklist because of his apolitical stance, thus making a new career possible for him. Was the accident a suicide? No one knows. The two other people in the car were unharmed.

Not long after Marian's death, Maria Byk died too. Ferdinand told me that by the end she was drinking Sterno when nothing else could be found to dull her inner pain. The younger Ferdinand buried her in the same grave as her husband, and he entered into his inheritance. He inherited the superb ring of the famous man; the furniture; the suits, which suited him perfectly once he had grown into them; four thousand books; and an identity.

Just like his Papa, every inch the Marian, said the directors. Yes, what a similarity! Ferdinand told me how easily he was accepted in the theatrical world.

From a mere boy with a laundry basket, walking out of a nameless basement apartment, he had returned as an educated young man, reinvented as an actor, as if in a fairy tale. As if he had negotiated himself a birthright with his charm and beauty. As if the professor as wizard had played with the energy that brings people together. The bit with the high school had been a declaration of love for a quite different fate.

It is a fact that Ferdinand adapted to this unbelievably mobile theatrical world with the agility of a chameleon. They had sashayed toward one another blindfolded, had smiled at one another as if they had known that they were perhaps related, by blood or marriage. Even before, with other people from distant times. An accident of birth, which Ferdinand simply put aside, because people believed much more in his flamboyant reincarnation. Where did the truth lie? In that time, on the stage of the times, where Ferdinand played his role, everyone looked about for the best possible conditions. Ferdinand Marian, Ferdinand Anton, had the same astrological profile, Leo, engraved in the ring Ferdinand now wore. Even their hands were the same.

Beautiful hands, a sign of character, I thought.

•

Tell me no tales. I have watched gigantic trees, observed how the leaves whisper among themselves, and remembered rumors, events, that would not rest.

Annemarie Albertine Böck, alias Maria Byk, had a daughter, Johanna, from her marriage with the well-known director Julius Gellner. Daughter and Jewish father had emigrated to England shortly before the war. Johanna was Ferdinand's age.

In the beginning, in the room of absolute truth, Ferdinand told the story:

After the war I dug up Johanna, "Joan Gellner," in London. We lived there together for some time.

Ten years later he introduced her to me as "my sister." The smoke from her cigarette extended her every sentence, and the hard liquor gave her voice a rasping whisper. She was said to have been pretty and jolly.

"Picking up anecdotes from the vanishing past" filled many hours long into the night.

On her last visit she had trouble clambering up the four flights. Small pitiless eyes peered from the bloated face, tired, gray, the old stories too, and it seemed to me she was about to cry. But nothing permitted that, least of all Ferdinand's domestic happiness. She was not yet old. One has little pity with young alcoholics, and she seemed to know that; nor had she asked for any.

And men? Men often react cruelly when a woman they once happily screwed around with debases herself and spoils the memory of the fun with undignified self-abandonment.

The Song of Irresponsibility

[O]ne of the girls, when she wasn't a girl anymore and hadn't
long been back from her honeymoon, went into the bathroom,
stood in front of the mirror, unbuttoned her blouse, took off her
bra and aimed her own father's gun at her heart...

—Javier Marías, *A Heart So White*

DURING THIS TIME I COULD HAVE DIED OF LOVE.

One day Ferdinand had appeared at my parents' house and said he would like to marry me. He did not ask for my hand in marriage. In a whispered tone my mother squeezed out: What? Already? So quickly? She was taken completely by surprise.

My father gazed darkly upon my future husband. Behind his forehead an opera of thoughts was playing itself out.

Why such a hurry? How on earth do you propose to feed a household?

Ferdinand puffed at his pipe and gave a friendly smile, pregnant with promise. The scene amused and inspired him. Then he launched. He told my father, with wonderful persuasiveness that had something magical about it, the fairy tale of earning one's bread. No one could compete with him at this.

With infectious excitement he reported his own unstoppable rise, told of the books on archeology that he was to write, decked out with photographs from his immense archive of pre-Columbian artifacts.

I was thrilled at the way Ferdinand leaned his head, the way he laughed, made my father laugh, the impassioned way he shaped and polished his stories.

One might label his charm insidious, his persuasiveness a wizard's. He did magic for Fritz *und* Adi, and both fell a wearied victim to his spell. My father, smiling and uncharacteristically pleased, suddenly tossed into the wind his realistic objections, which had been much more plausible than Ferdinand's dream dances; he shoved aside all warnings and logical barriers and thereby severed the last thread of reality.

The wedding in the civil registry was quite unceremonious, devoid of all solemnity, hastily gone through with, as if we had to keep an important appointment—the sailing of a ship, for example, which would not have taken us along were we not married. In reality we could not wait any longer, since I was growing more nauseated every day. I pretended to have eaten something disagreeable, but even without a confession my mother knew what was going on.

When Ferdinand and I returned from Vienna, where we had traveled on our honeymoon, my belly had rounded out, so my condition was obvious. But now we could cheerily talk about it, which would not have been possible before the wedding. I had wanted to get pregnant so that, in case of emergency, I could force a wedding and make a liar of my brother. When he first met Ferdinand, he had said in a dismissive tone: That one you will soon be rid of. Model Number: Windbag. He will take off one day…

I knew my father was not happy. I could feel how hard it had been for him to say yes. In his body language I read resignation: the way he sat folded into his desk chair, the desk a symbol of his earlier executive authority…And somehow he had to be thinking back on those days when he had fallen for Heinz the Listener. But this time the roles were reversed: Fritz the Listener had fallen for Ferdinand the Storyteller.

•

The baptism of our son Oliver was a beautiful little party. Father Dörfler, who had been my religious teacher at school, baptized Oliver in a simple Evangelical church. My mother was present; so were Ferdinand's mother, Erika, and Helga and Klaus, the godparents—both actors from Ferdinand's past.

Afterward we gathered in Adi and Fritz's apartment to celebrate. With baby Oliver in my arms I hastened into the living room to see my father, who had been waiting for us—to steal him from his isolation and show him the newly baptized child.

Adi set the table with the poppy setting that was designed by her father for Nymphenburg.

Today is a celebration! she laughed.

The kid doesn't see any of it, said Fritz.

In the middle, the vase with the roses, she continued, unperturbed.

Mother Erika cooked a zesty pork roast. From the kitchen, foreign to her, we heard loud altercations with herself: where on earth this and that was to be found.

Of course it isn't as if I was cookin' in my own kitchen. Every dish she set on the table was accompanied by this disclaimer.

With a flowered apron bound round her plump body, she stood throughout the meal at the end of the table, monitoring portions and making sure everyone got enough.

You're not eating anything, she said to me. You got to eat for two now, to keep your milk up. Oliver was drinking at my breast, and over and over the conversation got caught:

Yes, who does the little guy look like?

Seems to me he looks like Grandfather Marian. Helga and Klaus nodded in agreement. Blind as bats, they tapped their way into the Marian myth, and we laughed and nodded.

Yes, Ferdinand, it's you he looks like, not Beatrix, said Adi.

No, really, he looks more like a Mayan Indian, said Fritz, and Ferdinand beamed.

We had moved into an artist's apartment. A tall, bright living space with a gigantic north-facing window. Ivory light flooded into the room, no matter what the weather. Lined up next to the atelier were three small bedrooms. Marian's superb furniture joined the Biedermayer I had contributed from my dowry. When Ferdinand refashioned the bathroom into a darkroom, a Do Not Disturb sign was glued on the door, while, in the bathroom, photographs hung drying on a clothesline across the bathtub. Then I bathed Oliver in the kitchen sink. The diapers boiled in a gigantic pot on the gas stove. The remainder of the washing I dragged down four floors to the laundromat and back up again. Ferdinand was in charge of bringing the canisters with the heating oil up from the cellar.

And, with or without an invitation from us, guests fluttered in every night like moths. Massive numbers of cheap red wine bottles wandered up into our studio, full, and wandered back down, empty, with the drunken guests.

Ferdinand miraculously managed, despite the guests, to write his books about archeological studies of pre-Columbian art. Meanwhile I was running to the Academy of Art, already painting portrait commissions and earning the bulk of our money doing fashion shoots and film commercials. I had endless energy, making me so busy that my mother always said, My God, child, you have a hard life. That, however, I did not want to hear, and dissuaded her. We were happy.

When money came in from Ferdinand's publishers, he called it a pile, financial manna that showered down upon us. But, realistically, it was more of a modest sum.

In those days Ferdinand was on several movie-industry tracks. He played in one series called *As Far As Your Feet Will Carry You*. He wrote the script for the documentary *In Search of B. Traven*, the pseudonym used by the author of *The Treasure of the Sierra Madre*, which John Huston had made into a Humphrey Bogart movie. Traven had never shown his face, and his mysterious existence inspired all sorts of doubts, not least because he dragged a great many other pseudonyms through life with him. He first wrote his books in German.

I remember the uproar when, to everyone's amazement, Ferdinand dug him up in Mexico City and was even able to film him for a few seconds: an inquisitive expression, a pleading glance through an open door. Later, in this same Mexico, Ferdinand would seem almost as mysterious to me as B. Traven.

•

To round out our idyll, we rented what was known as a Schrebergarten, in one of Mr. Schreber's garden retreats, at the northern city limits of Munich. A little rectangle of land amid hundreds of identical others, with a little wooden house on it, a water faucet with a wooden barrel. Over and over there was shrieking when a child, playing with a boat, had bent too far over the barrel's rim, leaving nothing visible but a disappearing foot. Until we put an end to the terror by laying a top, weighted down with stones, across the barrel.

In the little garden, sunflowers bent over red currant bushes. Strawberries bordered a bed of radishes and kohlrabi. Tomatoes reddened along a fence. Peonies and larkspur. In the middle we planted a cherry tree; along the house wall trellis, apples and climbing roses. It smelled delicious, it wafted along, one heard the birds, shrill and silent. A parasol threw off its shadow skirt. When we were lucky and the neighbors tolerated it, we could dance with friends on the patch of grass in the moonlight, grill sausages, and have loud debates.

A hiccough sprang through the whispering; in the bushes there was rustling. Tripping over pots and beer steins, couples bumped into the cherry tree, stripped, and dunked themselves in the water barrel to sober up.

Slowly this nightly party billows past me, sexy and drunken, one's mouth full of suppressed laughter, heated discussions, communistic metaphors, stiletto heels sunk into soft ground, puking between berry bushes, and the sudden venom of the philistine chorus next door:

Now you've gone too far. You're disturbing the peace.

Time to shut the hell up, screamed someone over the fence, his voice heavy with beer. We gotta work tomorrow. Ya know, work? cried the voice once again, to remind us what it thought of us, us, the lazy artist riffraff.

Who would like to discuss this old, passed-away time with me, a time that was as natural for us as breathing? We made love in this wooden summerhouse and held a hand over each other's mouths to keep from laughing out loud.

·

Ferdinand learned ten Spanish words a day on the loo, and quite quickly, so it seemed to me, he spoke fluent Spanish. Once, before our time, he had gone on tour through South America with the Munich Kammerspiele ensemble, doing Schiller's *Kabale und Liebe*. There was a newspaper article about him: "I Was the Loftiest Ferdinand." In Peru he had to breathe from an oxygen bottle between appearances, because of the altitude of the City of Lima. That trip had been the midwife of his passion for archaeology.

This period was so thickly packed with events. One episode from Ferdinand's kaleidoscope, decipherable at the time only in part: a voluptuous young personage who rang our doorbell, rolled past me once I had opened the door for her, and stood in the middle of the studio. In a bag she was carrying a few bottles. She did not simply drop them off and depart; no, with an exhausted sigh, on account of the four flights of stairs, she flopped herself into a chair, as if the chair were made to measure for her to wait for Ferdinand. After a while she even sauntered around the room, impudent and crude, observed me, followed me with her eyes like a movie camera, watching what I was up to with the child or with the housework.

I offered her tea. She's fine, she's good, she gestured, and strolled over to Ferdinand's study. There she settled into Ferdinand's desk chair. With her small, plump hand, with its little fire-red nails, she held the whiskey pressed into her lap, so that it pushed her breasts up and they turned toward me, probing, like a second pair of eyes. Something like me was an unknown. But as for Ferdinand, him she must know well, I reflected, for she leaned back lazily, took a look over her shoulder, bent quite casually into his writings, and rustled playfully, quite intimately, with the papers. Everything else around her, me above all, she held firmly on her cold celluloid.

And Ferdinand finally appeared. They were only a few minutes out of synch. She stood up and they both muttered under their breath. The whiskey disappeared into a desk drawer. No money changed hands.

As the door fell to behind her, I asked: Who on earth was that?

Her? Oh, she is Mike's girlfriend, she works at the PX. The whiskey is a present from Mike. Incredibly generous.

Ferdinand took me into his arms and kissed me, and I quickly forgot everything that had shot through my head in her broad, saucy, voluptuous presence.

Her steps down the stairs took my thoughts away with them. I held Oliver on my arm, and I was happy. Love in itself is enough in this early phase of love.

Chaos Takes Over Order

IN 1960 THE AUSCHWITZ TRIALS TOOK PLACE IN FRANKFURT. The media provided exact reports, which brought the facts home to everyone in the most horrendous detail.

1961. The Wall split Berlin into East and West, and Germany into two halves, separated by an impenetrable barbed-wire border. The purpose was to block the massive western migration of qualified workers. Official propaganda spoke of an "anti-fascist protecting wall." The threat of the Cold War hung across the land. At the University of Frankfurt, Theodor Adorno and Max Horkheimer lectured on the "Dialectic of Enlightenment," spoke of emancipation from the paternalistic Nazi State, from its slanders against reality, from the "Guilty Generation." But *All are free to dance and enjoy themselves...*

21 June 1962. In a convalescing Germany, keeping the peace was the citizen's first duty. 10 o'clock: curfew. But young people were still strolling through the streets. Five student troubadours made music near a fountain beneath chestnut trees, on the Feilitzschplatz in Munich-Schwabing. A sickle moon hung in the sky, high above the musicians, also somewhere between the Frauenkirche and the Theresienwiese. A soft breeze stroked the skin, the dogs' fur, lifted creatures of the night aloft. Torpedo bugs raced into the light of the lanterns. Moths burned holes in their flight dress. Lovers squeezed into entrances, until little cries betrayed their presence. Cats waited optimistically in front of a

crack in a wall. No one could bring himself to go to sleep. It was perhaps the Fön, the warm wind that fans down from the mountains, what they call *scirocco* in Italy, *mistral* in Spain.

Chairs were already turned over on the tables of the inns, and yet the little group of students at the fountain beneath the chestnut trees still went on making music. They were playing Dixieland jazz, and now and then a Russian song. Around them gathered more and ever more young sleepless folks. They squandered their sensuality, touched a foot, an arm, shoulder, mouth, smiled at one another amid the joyous, foreign music, with all its possibilities for falling in love, for drunkenness, for drowning. In the sweet scent of this night, that belonged to everyone, there had been no omens. But then, suddenly, someone blew their top.

Keeping the peace, the citizen's first duty. Out of a window near the plaza, above the plaza, covered by the branches of the trees, a voice screamed, a shrill voice at the end of its tether:

Shut the hell up! Cut it out! You cut it out or I call the cops! Disturbing the peace!

Those beneath the trees—there were now perhaps a hundred of them—just wanted to hear their music. They had still not come to the end of their night, held one another by the hand, leaned on one another, swung, swayed to the beat of the notes.

Quit disturbing the peace!

Get lost, shut your trap, you square! some of them shouted back chaotically. Just plug your ears, you Nazi asshole!

But, in the event, police cars appeared and blocked the road to the plaza. The band played louder. The people shouted even more. All of a sudden cops were swarming everywhere, trying to bust up the crowd. The band played louder still.

Petty bourgeois pigs! Gestapo shitheads! shouted the young people—for whom all police were effectively Gestapo—and bunched up together. Buckets of water emptied themselves from windows onto lovebirds, onto the musicians, who could not stop playing. More and more people shoved and jostled around on the little plaza, more and more cops, more and more shouting.

You old Nazis! You fat right-wing pigs! Get your fat arses out of your offices! It's our turn! screamed the children of the great war, who were now young adults—screaming with the lungs of disobedience against the authoritarian state, screaming for emancipation from the paternalistic Nazi State.

Rocks flew, glass burst. Tussling and beating. Men and women were stuffed willy-nilly into police cars.

It takes only one spark to send the frustrations of the whole world burning from door to door.

There was no end in sight. The first night led to the next day. Thousands of reinforcements pushed their way in, filled the streets, lit cars afire, threw rocks, sat on tram tracks. Truly thousands. They increased like the serpent head of the Hydra. Fires burned in the streets, military cordons drew into formation, supported by police on horseback.

Aha! Those musicians had played Russian songs. A samovar had even been found in one of the students' digs. *All are free to dance and enjoy themselves.* But...

Whoever dared not go outside, wanted to keep out of it, not get mixed up with it, saw the ballet of uprising as agitation, as information on the screen at home, day and night. The rebellion did not remain isolated in Munich; it ran, it raced across the German land mass to France and issued an invitation to join in. The bush drums beat for the revolutionaries, the provocateurs, the dissatisfied, the virtuous and the vicious.

Ferdinand and I were in the thick of things. He felt in his element. We were always to be found on the street with the demonstrators, who had formed themselves into a single global thought.

The future is ours; away with you old buzzards!

Adorno-Horkheimer: Enlightenment as Mass Deception. Opposites are one in their enthusiastic obedience to the rhythm of the iron system...

Sartre, the leading interpreter of the postwar generation's worldview, wrote in *The Humanism of Existentialism*: "In the beginning is man, he shows himself, steps onstage, and defines himself only later."

To this day it seems to me as if our apartment was the center of the Happening, as if the Revolution had found its starting point there, among us in the studio, at Ferdinand Marian's oak table, surrounded by Ferdinand's 4000 books, the manifestos of Che Guevara, Sartre, Brecht.

From my little kitchen came bourgeois odors, of security, the legacy of my turbulent childhood. Nothing will change. It will pass. Robust reality holds the threads of happiness firmly in both hands.

•

Ferdinand sat in the alcove of his room and raged across the keys with two middle fingers. At equal intervals he puffed little clouds of smoke from his pipe, like angry thoughts. The smoke signals flew across the roof, out and away through the open hinged windows, where he was reflected many times over, as if in an Escher drawing. I stood in front of my easel, painted, and sang my beloved Brecht and Eisler songs.

Eil, Liebster, zu mir, teurer Gast,	*Hurry to me, lover, precious guest,*
Wie ich keinen teurern find.	*More precious than any I know.*
Doch wenn du mich im Arme hast,	*But when you have me in your arms*
Dann sei nicht so geschwind.	*Then don't be so hasty*
Nimm's von de Pflaumen im Herbste	*Take it from the plums in autumn*
Wo reif zum Pflücken sind...	*That are ripe for the plucking...*

Scarcely had Ferdinand sat for a few minutes when he jumped up, ran through the little room, in search of his brilliance and of a bottle of Underberg, which he had promoted to his medical elixir; to calm the nerves, neutralize the stomach, refresh the course of his thoughts. Back again to the desk. By evening, after twenty Underbergs, all scruples had been gulped down, and in a quest—this time for relaxation—there flowed vast quantities of red wine with many unavoidable and avoidable friends, who were all in agreement, who theorized with one another, castigated the *Scheissstaat*, the petty-bourgeois philistines, the fat right-wingers, the former Nazis. These Nazis in turn had been cleansed of their National Socialist past by the Allies, with a piece of paper, a questionnaire, as if by magic. Now they were once again in high office, and outside, in front of the door, the Moloch of the Sixties movement grew incessantly. Thus it began.

I myself came from a family of political freethinkers, but back then I had little time for political thought, free or not. I juggled between Baby Oliver, my film and photo shoots, and my painting.

My father, who had given up striving for his own advantage, considered the political turmoil a stage play doomed to failure. The vanity of his sick body gave him insight into the vanity of the physical world.

Human beings always blame the government. But the blame always lies with human beings themselves. Egotists, wicked liars. Fritz continued with Goethe:

| Er nennts Vernunft, gebrauchts allein | He calls it reason, and uses it only |
| Um tierischer als jedes Tier zu sein | To be more beastly than any beast |

At any rate, revolutionaries were squatting in our studio every night, passing the time with feckless quotes on Renewal, with red wine, beer, and clouds of tobacco smoke. It was interesting to climb the four flights up to our place. One always met kindred spirits. I too found it stimulating, was never tired, loved it.

One of my favorite visitors in those days was Konstantin of Bavaria. We were very close friends and very, very distant relatives, owing to the extramarital creativity which led to my grandfather, who had his father in common with Sissi of Austria. Konstantin loved to take part in our socialist salons, to charge his batteries as a right-wing politician and as a journalist. It was always a lively dust-up, and there were plenty of curiosity-seekers. When we ever managed to sleep, I have no clue.

Il Commandante, Che Guevara, was our revolutionary hero. There were photos and newspaper clippings of him and of Fidel Castro stuck in picture frames, taped to the front door. Ferdinand shared Che's anti-imperialistic ideas, and they both loved the writings of Federico García Lorca and César Vallejo, and many others, whose Spanish mother tongue had become Ferdinand's favorite language.

Ferdinand, who was always looking for masculine *comrados* and collected them, found one more in Che Guevara, the *guerrilleroheroico*. Not that war was anything but repellent to him, but he loved heroes, and their songs as well:

Ich bin aus Havana	I'm from Havana,
Meine Mutter war eine Weisse	My mother was a white woman
Sie sagte oft zu mir:	She often said to me:
Mein Kind, verkauf' Dich nicht	My child, don't sell yourself
Für ein Paar Dollarnoten	For a few dollar notes,
Wie ich es tat	As I did.

He sang. As naively as a child he took in everything, as raw material, even the nights—which let themselves be sculpted at his pleasure—and words like "Havana," "Tabak," "Brecht," "Revolution."

Back then Ferdinand often traveled to East Germany, meaning: from the Munich train station directly to the E.A. Seemann publishing house in Leipzig, and back, with no detours. For the People's Police, the *Volkspolizei*, the Vopo, did not permit any pleasure walks. You had to tell them your exact destination.

His books were published in this very house in Leipzig, in exquisite classical style, and his polemical works were greatly esteemed in the Eastern Bloc. It was Ferdinand's view that so many things just had to be better over there: they may not have had our affluence, but, in exchange, they had ideals worth striving for.

And indeed his publishers celebrated him like a king. Clearly Ferdinand had chosen an East German publishing house over any Western competitor. For him, as a literary man, this made plenty of sense, but one could not help noticing that the East German government had no respect for freedom of speech. The motto of the KPD: Keep your mouth shut, just be sure to keep your mouth shut. Two men, one informant.

I once went along on one of these trips. There was a regular command performance, a costume party, like in the picture by Paul Klee, *Two Men Meet, Each Believing the Other to Be of Higher Rank*, where two men bow deeply and awkwardly, with an eighteenth-century sweep of the arm. Each imagines the other a personification of his ideal desires.

Jealousy ruled the roost. The West had it so much better economically. At the door of every halfway upper-end restaurant stood a Vopo operative, who allowed only foreign guests into the establishment. As they went past, the East Germans threw brief, angry glances at the door closed to them. I found it terrible and never again traveled to East Germany with Ferdinand.

Since he was constantly commuting back and forth, it was unavoidable that he would be offered the deceitful role of informant. He once showed me an expensive watch they had presented him with, clearly bait. But he reconsidered. He found it degrading to sniff about in the milieu of politics.

After all these Leipzig trips, Ferdinand had made several friends there. Everyone regarded everyone else hesitantly, filled with mistrust, lifting their masks carefully only after some time. Whispering, behind closed doors, furious, red in the face, full of fear and anger, they enlightened him. They castigated the Nazis who had crept in everywhere in East Germany, who pushed plum posts each other's way, used Marx and Engels as a decorative alibi, behaved even more corruptly than their colleagues in the West. A popular underground proverb had it that the acronym for the (East) German Democratic Republic, "DDR," stood for "der dumme Rest," "the dumbass dregs," and this harmonized exactly with his friends' sentiments. Ferdinand came home more and more sobered, scornfully turned his back on inter-German politics.

Elixir of Personal Freedom

SOMETIMES, WHEN MY MOTHER HAD ERRANDS, and my father was alone, I visited him with my little Oliver. The stillness stood in the apartment like a piece of furniture. Oliver's presence brought noise with it, so that my father seemed more frightened than glad. I sat the little fellow on Fritz's lap, yet I could not let go of him, not for a moment, for my father did not dare to hold him himself. It took just a momentary touch, and little Oliver burst out crying. Once he had calmed down, and was contemplating his grandfather, he would smile and speak: Ta ta ta ta. Then Fritz would smile too, from far, far away, across to this child.

What on earth will become of you? he would say.

Perhaps a racecar driver, I answered. He loves cars.

Vrumm vrumm, went Oliver at the sound of the word "car."

The three of us seemed imprisoned in the room, until my mother's key made a sound in the front-door lock, simultaneously unlocking our captivity.

My mother left the house for a few hours. She was visiting Aunt Fränzi, her mother's sister, who had lived in Sofia. Now she lived here in Munich. Because she was so old, the Bulgarian authorities had allowed her to depart. Old people could slip through the Iron Curtain. Those they did not want to keep. Ballast for the state.

Aunt Fränzi journeyed to us by train. Sewn up in the hem of her skirt, a fortune in diamonds lay hidden. During the long trip she sat on two antique, uncommonly valuable Persian carpets. On her lap she held Ingres's "Portrait of a Lady." The portrait she declared to be a picture of her grandmother; the Persian carpets, her customary travel pillow. These few objects and a small suitcase were all she was allowed to take with her.

When my glorious old great-aunt Fränzi came to us, she was hunched and used up by Communist misanthropy. Now she blossomed. She liberated the diamonds from her skirt hem and negotiated a better life for herself. She rode a taxi to the dealers, hobbled from opportunity to better opportunity, leaning on her walking-stick, until she decided the price was right.

Adi had visited Aunt Fränzi and her husband, Uncle Methodi Popov, in the twenties in Sofia. Methodi and his brother Kyril Popov remain proud sons of Bulgaria to this day. Methodi was a botanist, Kyril a mathematician. According to family lore, they won Nobel Prizes. There are two streets in Sofia named after them.

Aunt Fränzi and Methodi had a close friendship with the Bulgarian king. Methodi, for many years the ambassador at Berlin, tended to be the more quiet and thoughtful, while Aunt Fränzi conversed fluently in nine languages and told superb stories. With her enormous gift she could talk to anyone. And now she lived with us and did little deals with her diamonds. She was very mysterious, and no one knew what was what with her fortune.

She acted like a poker player, let no one see her cards, which in turn greatly irritated Fritz. He was also afraid that he would have to support her financially at the end.

Having grown mistrustful through the dreadful years of Communism, she did not really trust our money either.

Boy, these are thin, she growled, rubbing the Deutschmark notes between her thumb and forefinger.

Auntie moved into an apartment in the Waldfriedhofstrasse, Forest Cemetery Street, but she found the Cemetery part unacceptable and promptly rechristened her address Waldstrasse, Forest Street. Somehow she managed to strike up a sort of friendship with the mailman, and, for a few "thin notes," her mail was correctly delivered to her, despite the wrong street name.

With me Aunt Fränzi only spoke English, so I would learn it, but I merely managed to mangle it after my own fashion. My main language at school was not English but Latin. My mother laughed with pleasure. She used her French less for conversation, more for citing sayings she could easily keep in mind.

> *Voulez-vous with me pousser,*
> *Dans la rue the tree-lined way,*
> *Non, monsieur, it cannot être*
> *Mon Papa is sitting at fenêtre.*

At this Aunt Fränzi had to laugh along, and countered:

> *Ach, Frau Kommerzienrat,*   *Oh, Madam Commerce Secretary*
> *Ich bin ganz desperat*   *My anguish is quite extraordinary,*

Warum gibt's heuer keinen Jour?   *Why is there not one lovely jour?*
Ach, teurer Freund, die Zeit   *Oh, my dear friend, old Time*
ist bitter: *is bitter,*
Was einmal war, kommt nie retour   *What once was, never comes retour*

Between Fritz and Fränzi the discourse was at a most intellectual level. He did not particularly enjoy her company, so every conversation led to a competition where each tried to trump the other with the most lofty theme he could dream up. Auntie spoke Italian, Fritz interpolated Latin. They were never in agreement, and after a while they would knot themselves up into a quarrelsome dust-up between know-it-alls. Someone, whether a guest or my mother, had to break in and change the subject completely:

Here, look at this superb cake, who would like whipped cream?

But the conversation went best with Ferdinand. Fränzi was happy that he spoke Spanish and that she could help with his ongoing learning.

After the Russians occupied Bulgaria, Aunt Fränzi had been forced to undertake a detailed study of lower-class lifestyles. In her feudal villa every room housed large families with whom one also had to share the bath. She recounted how people would wash their face in the toilet; meanwhile a privy with a ditch was erected in the garden, the kind they were used to from living out in the country.

Those years of poverty had accustomed Aunt Fränzi to narrow coexistence with strange people under the most unhygienic circumstances, and she could no longer change her ways.

At my age one no longer changes anything, she said. Which must be why she so seldom bathed. Too strenuous. Though she did perfume and powder herself with composure, like people during the Rococo era. And since she was not tender, never had been, one kept at a finely perfumed distance with all the foreign languages, immersed in intellectual conversation.

She always wore wonderful hand-stitched lingerie, whose lace décolleté insert concealed her aged bosom.

Always good lingerie. If you get mixed up in an accident, it is your calling card. The lingerie will speak for itself, and people will treat you well.

During her last ten years she lived large and carefree. And then, without falling ill, just a little forgetful and very old, she died in her Empire bed, free, with no attachments, like a cat.

•

Adi had been taking care of two people, and now only of Fritz, very much an invalid.

On her way home she bought a bunch of peonies. Red and pink. She unlocked the door.

Fritz, I'm back, she called out into the sepia vestibule.

While she laid her keys and purse on a side table, her eyes adjusted to the twilight in the apartment. First the flowers, her beloved flowers, they needed water. Without taking off her hat, still in her coat, she walked to the kitchen. On the way there she looked for a moment into the living room. Fritz was sitting in his chair in front of the desk by the window.

Hello, I'm back again. Ah, you're sleeping, she murmured.

She crept back into the kitchen on tiptoe, quietly opened the glass cupboard, chose a crystal vase, and cautiously filled it with water. The drawer creaked as it opened. She fished for the flower shears. Every peony stem was trimmed a half-centimeter, the lower leaves snipped from the shaft. With great care she joined one flower to the other in the vase.

It's a dream, she said, as she placed the last stem. With the bouquet pressed close to her face, breathing in the scent, she went the few steps back from the kitchen into the living room, to Fritz, and put the flowers on the right side of his desk.

His face leaned toward the window, with his chin on his left shoulder. The closed eyes gave an effect of nakedness without the glasses, which lay before him on the desk on top of a crookedly creased piece of paper. His hands had been folded, it seemed; released from the exertion of holding each other, they now leaned softly on one another, like sleepers.

Fritzl, said Adi and tenderly laid her hand on his shoulder. Fritzl?

Across his mouth, slightly open, played the inclination of a smile, making half his face seem broader, softer, as if it had lost its composure. His left arm gave way and the hand glided into the seat of the chair, with a gentle *z-zs-zs-sst*. My mother looked at the open hand, the only part of his body that had moved, if quite powerlessly, and she could not pull herself away. She lost herself in contemplation. A mental vacuum throttled her.

Yes, her glance followed this hand that had glided from his lap with that quiet *z-zs-zs-sst* and now seemed to point motionlessly at something below; her glance followed it into the dimness on the floor between the chair and the windowsill.

There, something glimmered, little bits of glass, from a shattered whole, a small glass, perhaps an ampule. She looked for some time at the shards, to be certain, stared, unable to tear herself loose, stared for quite a while, until she slowly went around the chair, bent down, and, cupping one hand to form a receptacle, collected the glass fragments into it with the other.

Once every sliver of glass was in her hand, Adi opened the window, bent out, and with all her might hurled the bits deep into the evergreens, as if she were tossing a ball. Gunpowder gray sky, on the threshold of night.

The drawer of the desk stood a little open: one centimeter, perhaps.

Fritzl, I must bring you to bed. You have to lie down, said Adi.

She went to the telephone and dialed, staring into Nowhere, past Fritz in the chair, past the peonies in the vase.

Hello, hello, Ferdinand, she said. Ferdinand, can you come over and help me? Fritz has fallen asleep in the chair. I'd like to carry him into his bed.

After the door closed behind Ferdinand, leaving my mother alone again, Fritz lay in his half of the marital bed. Adi took off her clothes and folded them on the chair, went into the bathroom and wove her hair into a braid for the night.

She looked into the mirror. Tears welled up across her eyelids, without any sobbing, silently, dripped from the edge of her chin down into her décolletage, onto her breast.

After Adi had put out the lights, petted the dog, she lay down in bed with Fritz. Her head on the pillow, tears running from the corners of both eyes, over her cheekbones into her ears.

A spirit light hurried across the bedroom ceiling. The sound of a slamming car door shot up from the courtyard. Ruff, Ruff, the bellowing of Mr. Wagner's dog. Steps hurrying off. Through the sieve of night, the noises of the street dripped into the room. Adi held in her hand the folded sheet of paper, the one from Fritz's desk, beneath his eyeglasses, the letter: it was an empty sheet. She pressed it to her heart. She closed her eyes, and the room filled with the stale scent of peonies, while her breast heaved and contracted, her breath streamed in and out. Fritz's voice, clear and very close:

Beloved Adi,

We have been together so long that I can keep nothing from you.

You know my thoughts.

I want to go now.

I cannot go on.

Doctor Schäfer says I should not miss the moment when I still have the strength to open the drawer and pull the ampule from the right rear corner where it is hidden.

Since 1943.

I could no longer completely close the drawer.

Also the ampule slipped out of my hand after I broke it open.

You know how difficult it is for me to control my numb hands.

I am glad you stayed away a while longer, so that I could find a quiet moment.

Adilein, thank you for all your help.

It was a good life, enough excitement for two.

Now I am letting it all go.

Never wanted to grow old.

Kiss Anita, Uli, and Beatrix.

Don't wake me.

I've had enough.

"Fate shuffles the cards, and we play."

Leave me the last word.

Your

Fritz

•

A little group of friends, a bit of family, we sat in the Aubergine, a French fish restaurant, the first of its kind in Munich after the war. We toasted one another, hoisted our glasses to Fritz, our father, our friend Fritz, to his memory.

Ah, that Fritz. He certainly could tell superb stories.

My God, his African tales, said Aunt Gitta.

A coryphaeus in agriculture, said Uncle Schmelzle.

Unfortunately I did not get along with my father, said Uli.

But you're very much like him, said Aunt Esther.

Loved you children all alike, said Adi. Aunt Gitta said: But his darling was Beatrix.

Anita sobbed.

Even so: I do not know of anyone else with such a feeling for honor and justice. Unbelievable, said Uli, still grappling with the Oedipus question.

Superb, the fish soup. Fritz would have liked it too.

Oh, yes, if anyone enjoyed eating well, it was Fritz. He liked beer, but he knew a lot about wine, our Fritz, and about beautiful women. Never looked away from you, though, Adi. You were the most beautiful.

My mother was wearing her French felt hat, the one Fritz had brought her from Bordeaux in 1941, during the war, way back then, as a parting gift. Shortly before he headed out to join Rommel in North Africa, he had come home one last time on leave, to say goodbye. Uli was away with the Hitler Youth, but Fritz could still hug me and Anita one more time, kiss Adi one more time.

Mother's brown hat, sporting a satin sash of the same color. Two guinea-hen feathers, gray with white dots, presumably from our own guineas at the farm, protruded jauntily on one side. She wore her black wool suit, in mourning, as was fitting. But it was the hat she wore for her Fritz, who had so loved giving presents.

Adi had red cheeks from the wine and from the general sense of relief. In the candlelight she looked like a young girl at her birthday party. Fritz did get the last word, giving her and himself back their freedom. For him the worst thing about illness had been the miserable dependency. His will was the true cripple.

Next to my mother sat Doctor Schäfer, Fritz's doctor and best friend during the final years. Every week they played chess, philosophized about books they read together, talked politics, and quarreled. Dr. Schäfer smiled to himself complacently. He wished to celebrate my father's end as a triumph, for his patient and for himself too. Friend, doctor, human being, who values quality of life more than mere existence. That my father had listened to him, preferred quality of life to quantity of years, must have pleased him. We were all agreed that Dr. Schäfer knew my father very well. They had nothing from the past in common, so Fritz could present his life to the doctor as he saw fit, and both could weigh together the still-open possibilities of a future. Schäfer, in turn, entrusted my mother with Fritz's deepest secrets, and, through this cunning provocation, gave her back her strength and great freedom.

To our surprise she became a world traveler. After Father's dog, Lexi, died, she did not want any more pets, so that nothing, at least no living duty, could hinder her freedom.

Our small group of mourners. The family intimate, the friends close. Silent lips moved in a toneless orchestra. A tragedy pushed the curtain aside.

Reality becomes an illusion, which in turn becomes each person's reality. Grieving, so we can love.

Each person—each for himself, each in his own way—drew a strong emotional energy from the grief at the loss of the father, the friend, Fritz. My mother wove thoughts as fluid as milk. Fritz took one last bow and tendered his regards.

Then we said goodbye, embraced, kissed one another on the lips, the cheeks, kissed and blew kisses and promised not to become strangers, not just on Fritz's account, no, also to keep our promise.

Borrowed from the light of the street lamps outside, we saw customers still sitting in the window of the Aubergine, their faces red with wine.

Above us dog-shaped clouds chased out past the stars. Our steps laughed on the asphalt. We turned one last time to wave, watched friends driving off.

Two hours later we were all, all fourteen of us, unbelievably ill from the delectable fish soup we had feasted upon in Fritz's honor.

Fritz almost managed to have the last word, one last time.

•

At the funeral banquet Ferdinand sat quite still, uncharacteristically still, lost in his thoughts, in the silent habit of his pipe ritual. This time he did not run the program of his magical reminiscences, the analogues from life, which he had formed from theatre pieces and books into scenes in which he played all the roles and thus entranced society. He was temporarily forgotten, being a new arrival in this intimate circle.

My fragile father, although carried off by the illness, had held Ferdinand firmly on the strings of his authority, like a marionette. He had called him a day-milker, with a cape of jesting and a wishbone of truth, often saying things like:

One should drink only to celebrate, not when one works.

When a master falls into depression, he becomes a dilettante.

Yet Fritz, who liked Ferdinand very much, loved his insouciance, something so foreign to Fritz. At the same time it felt frightening, for Ferdinand's behavior had something arrogant about it. My father was both fascinated with and alienated by Ferdinand's ability to outdo successive exaggerations until they mysteriously concentrated themselves into something that could pass for truth. Fritz very soon discovered that the peacock that pecks from one's hand is possessed by demons. And perhaps even because of all these weaknesses, transparent to him as tools for the art of survival, Fritz loved Ferdinand. He took Ferdinand in, held his sheltering hand over him. Fritz's presence protected Ferdinand from himself.

At the funeral banquet table Ferdinand sat quite still amidst our chattering party. When I squeezed his hand, he did not respond. He was lost, far off in his thoughts. Perhaps Fritz's death had made him feel like an unprotected child who had not known this type of fear before, because he had never experienced the protection of a benevolent authority. Fritz's presence had forced him into bourgeois respectability: husband, father.

My mother had called Ferdinand and asked him to help her carry Fritz to the bedroom.

Your father is incredibly heavy. I almost didn't manage to get him into his bed.

Nothing more was said when Ferdinand returned.

He had carried a dead man. My father had been dead, right there on the chair, when my mother first found him. Ferdinand knew, and it numbed him.

The ampule Fritz had kept hidden in his desk drawer since the war? Officers wore the little glass tab around their necks and if captured could decide for themselves: Should I end my life, or do I surrender myself to the enemy? One was master over one's fate. He must have held onto this thought since long before the debilitating illness had made itself perceptible—being master of the situation, not feeling at anyone's mercy, not trusting anyone else to overrule his will. Where his fate was concerned, he would always have the last word.

And I always thought my father died with dignity, fully conscious. The thought of helping him never occurred to anyone. He did not want that. He was no gambler. He did not want to hand Fate any cards—his life least of all—never wanted it to come down to that. He often read his Schopenhauer and was firmly convinced that everything we generally call our existence is illusory.

Fritz rode a camel toward the fire of the sun, along a jacaranda-blue path, amid the fragrance of anise, cinnamon, and saffron, carrion vultures on an indefinable patch of hill; rode onward into the orange sea of sand, the skeleton of a gigantic dragon, rode toward this hot sphere that rolled up high behind an oasis. Bedouins waited there beneath the palms. They bowed in greeting. He greeted them back, saw the falcon on the gloved hand, stretching its claws beneath its wings, the golden ring in its gaze. He heard the leaping, crackling heat that devoured him into its fire, in the slow motion of an instant.

Bob

A WEEK OF GLADSOME DAYS, poisonous green spring.

In the atelier the window stood ajar, the room full of day. A breeze wafted in occasional traffic noise from the intersection, children's laughter and screams from the playground. The sun dozed somewhere in the back of the roofs. Oliver had command over the atelier floor, upon which he built a mighty Lego tower, while I stood with my easel inside his play fence to paint, so that he could not disturb me, not splash around in my oils. At the other end of the studio, where the ceiling was lower, Bob lay on a sofa, immersed in a cookbook, his elbows sunk in a cushion.

Bob, our cook, emitted a hmmm, clicking his tongue.

That's what I'm cooking tonight. You like goulash?

Ferdinand had discovered Bob on Ludwigstrasse. He had stopped his car when he noticed a curious character who was busying himself behind a VW bus with a huge knife in his hand. They exchanged greetings. Bob grinned and lifted the lid of the soup pot that was bubbling on a gas camping stove.

Bob had just come from Spain, via Turkey and North Africa. In the back of his bus, next to a small place to sleep, was a jumble of vases, busts, pots, carpets, pictures. Germany was the final stop before he sailed back to New York to open an antique shop.

When the soup was ready, the two new simpaticos sat on the curb: two stools, a little table, slurping broth, drinking wine. And since they understood one another right away, Ferdinand brought Bob home with him so he could have a proper bath.

After his bath Bob simply stayed with us, as if by prearrangement, and cooked the most wonderful dinners. And we loved Bob. He was tall and sinewy, with a shaven head, soft, adorable features, reminiscent of a koala bear. He looked into the vestibule mirror with a satisfied air, striking an athletic pose and tensing his biceps. If caught at it, he gestured with his hand, put his arm around one's shoulder, and laughed:

Not bad, hmm…damned good-looking people.

Every Saturday Mother Erika puffed up the stairs to us to clean the apartment. Her shopping bag was full of sausage and ham, bread and pretzels for us, and a thick slab of meat. Scarcely had Erika closed the door behind her when Bob posed her, too, in front of the mirror, tied her apron around her portly girth, and drew her close to him, with her shamefacedly defending herself the whole time:

Cut it out! Cut it out! Oh, heavens, no, ain't…!

Damned good-looking, Bob would laugh, and finally let her go.

Bob was lighthearted and full of kindness. He moved quietly, supple as a tomcat, through rooms and through hearts. He could be a wonderful listener, so everyone told him everything. He collected not only objects but also stories, people, fates, recipes.

Sometimes Bob disappeared for days. At first I was very concerned, but Ferdinand calmed me; I was still so naive. Bob had, in fact, wandered off to dive into the gay scene. Then, after a few days, he would return to us, whistling contentedly as he stomped up the stairs, gliding back into our fried-potato idyll with artful elegance, his eyes still a little red from his excesses, but his smile once more intimate, gentle, good-natured, smirking at the banality of his outing. Sometimes he brought along a Peter or Hans or Martin, whom he lovingly added to his list of culinary tributes.

Leaving aside his gift for preparing exquisite dishes, I felt myself protected by Bob. In the larger sense he seemed to keep watch over the mysterious lexicon of life itself. Through the wrong end of the telescope he kept watch over situations, conflicts, states of mind, quarrels, love. And, viewed from this perspective, in their reduced form, completely insuperable difficulties were much less threatening.

Not as definitively as my father, yet in a similar way, Bob's presence tamed Ferdinand's craving for excess. Secretly he longed for honor, for bourgeois respectability, but could not carry it out, or could carry it out only with the greatest effort, in everyday life. He could not resist alcohol at any time of day, but as evening approached it practically screamed for him, and the bourgeois corset flew all the way out the window.

Bob protected our marriage, in which my organized domesticity and the mess of Ferdinand's drunken optimism butted heads. Often there were tensions between us that no one could decipher, let along solve. At those times Bob cooked superb dishes for us, like his Asiatic chicken soup. I would sing one of my songs, we would start dancing, and end up bursting into laughter, the weight dissolved.

First thing in the morning Bob went off to the market, holding Oliver's hand, while I ran to photo shoots to earn our daily bread. Ferdinand parked at his desk, puffing ashen mushrooms from his pipe and writing away on his books about pre-Columbian art, his whiskey bottle and the little bottles of Underberg always within easy reach.

One morning I woke up, the air around me, as always, a stale fog of the previous evening's tobacco and alcohol. As I went to open the window, my body felt the way it had felt once before. A little nausea, heavy breasts, and sweet expectation within me.

Ferdinand, I whispered into his ear, full of dreams: I'm pregnant.

Immediately he was wide awake.

How lovely, my darling. Of course, with a stud like you've got, even the sofa is probably pregnant, he laughed, springing from the bed and whirling me through the room and down the hall, to wake Bob with the glad tidings.

Bob, I'm pregnant again! I called out.

Bolstered in his passive masculinity by becoming a father for the second time, Ferdinand seized the opportunity to celebrate once more with the colorful crew that hung out at our place, a decision that released a corresponding flood of alcohol. Drinking was the correct response to all events, joyous as well as miserable.

Whether the evening had begun on a note of "pre-Columbian mysteries," or on "Beatrix is pregnant once again," or on "I have signed a book contract," or politics, whichever it was, his passion to return to his gods flared up within him in direct proportion to the number of bottles.

His figurines and *idoles* from the pre-Columbian period were at the center of our lives. Ferdinand's stories recounted orgiastic blood sacrifices, boundless vindictiveness of the gods. He seemed to feel himself an ambassador, assigned to clarify the facts, demystify the legends. He was obsessed with the mission of ripping History free from her anonymity. Compared with pre-Columbian history, the Greek temples, the idealization of the human body, the decadent frescoes of life in Pompeii and Herculaneum were signs of a far-too-idyllic worldview.

Ferdinand, his pipe now in his mouth, now in his hand, carried the visitors off with him. He read to us from his manuscript:

The temple centers molder away in the moist green grave of the jungle, and the natives give the same answer to every probing question: Quién sabe? Who knows? A romantic, Alfred P. Maudslay, was the first to make his way through the barely accessible forests, between 1881 and 1894, taking plaster casts of memorials and dragging many original pieces back to England with him. But it was gum-chewing that really shocked the palaces and temples of the Maya from their slumber. Searching for chicozapote trees, the Chicleros found a great many ruins, and that gave fresh impetus to get to the root of their origin, their mystery, and their downfall.

Ferdinand had devoured the heart of Mexico with all his passion, and he dreamed of breathtaking hills of stone, covered with thick, thorny bush, waiting for him to excavate them. And so he lay in wait, in an agony of longing for the foreign land that called out to him, saw the restless demons of the past in the shape of bats, flying out of the darkness of the abandoned ruins into the great ballroom of the night sky.

Do you want to see the Jaguar Temple?

No one wanted to answer no. And there would have been no point. The guests were his audience, his listeners; once again, they could not have wished for better theater, for any play presented with such passion.

I was proud of Ferdinand's knowledge and simply took care of the cheese and bread and wine and wine.

Do you want to see the Jaguar Temple?! The most beautiful example of Toltec architecture? Ferdinand called out. His tongue was already heavy, his head nonetheless light, full of triumph over everything banal. His collar wide open, his sleeves rolled up, he ran about the room gesticulating, Marian's ring on his finger, his pipe now in the corner of his mouth, now in his fist; held figures in the light of the lamp, rummaged for fragments in a box, to let samples share his podium. Already his disobedient tongue was only clumsily following the obsessed arrangement in his head. His wayward thoughts were betraying the burning heat of his mission. Photographs were passed around the circle of friends, parasites, lovers, people magnetically attracted to Ferdinand. Still more liquor, still more wine.

Ferdinand called out the eightfold echo of the cultic ball field. Sat with the Toltec dignitaries by the plumed serpents, the symbol of their power. Lifted his glass, lost himself in the description of a relief decorated with skulls like a deadly menace. In the form of a ribbon, it encircled the plaza, whose echo could carry even a whisper as far as 150 meters, in the midst of which stood the high temple, the Castillo.

The deadly breath of this lost history hovers over the plaza, he cried out.

And then, with no particular connection:

Mexican children play with skeletons, not dolls.

We were all silent. His thoughts leapt forward; little white clouds from his pipe hung in the space like wrathful incense.

He wove the names, every number, sites, symbols, gods, their place, the falling shadows, the temples, pillars, above them bas-reliefs, warriors in splendid uniforms, their eyes white mussels, the pupils black tar.

He fell into the rhythmic chant of a chorus:

> *1000 pillars, beneath the hot sky, pressed in upon by the restless jungle.*
> *9 landings of the pyramids, the nine heavens of the Toltecs*
> *91 stairs*
> *4 cardinal directions*
> *364 days and 1 day*
> *1 further stair that bears the Sacred*
> *adding up to the number of days in a solar year*
> *52 ornamental caskets, on each side of a substructure*
> *again a number, a one-year bundle*
> *52 solar years, the Castillo, the great pyramid of Chizen Iza*
> *built to honor Quezalcoatl–Kukulcán*
> *petrified symbol of the Toltec worldview.*

Outside, in front of the window, lay night. Silvery clouds, a dragon skeleton, hovered above the chimneys.

Have you got any of the goulash left? And bring some bread too.

Between the mountains of photos lay *idoles*, ceramic figurines so powerful in effect that they seemed life-sized. The jade mask of a priest, staring wrathfully at us. Between fragments, a little flute in the form of a bird, a tapir no larger than a walnut.

One o'clock in the morning. The guests had said goodnight. The goulash sat on the table, grown cold. Ferdinand stood in the middle of the studio, his right arm around Bob's shoulder to steady himself, in his left hand his pipe to gesticulate with. He had taken off his sweat-drenched shirt, his breast heaved and sank in little gusts, beads of sweat stood on his forehead. He started to hum, and then the words chiseled themselves into relief: the old song of Yucalpeten, "The Pearl at the Throat of the World." He sang, he sobbed, a tributary of tears and sweat ran into his verse:

> *Yucalpetén, Yucalpetén*
> *Everything is over*
> *Everything is silent*
> *The Indio cries*
> *His tears trickle deep into the earth*
> *The sanctified earth*
> *Yucalpetén Yucalpetén*
> *Everything passes away*
> *Everything is silent*

As I took one last look into the studio, already in my nightgown, everything in the room, the furniture, the books, seemed as fragile as his *idoles*, as the exotic objects that meant so much to Ferdinand. Nothing was what it seemed. Not Ferdinand, who was snoring on the blue sofa in the center of the room. Not the chair in the corner, with the outlines of a figure, a glowing cigarette.

Goodnight, Beatrix. That's his way, melancholy, said Bob, and he turned around to me so I could see his face.

You'll have another beautiful child, I know it.

Do stay with us, Bob, I thought—what will happen when you are gone? Archangel Bob. You understood it without my having to explain.

Everything will turn out right in the end. If it's not right, it's not the end.

Sympathy for the Object
of Contempt

THE ROOM FULL OF DAY.

The door fell into its catch as she left. Erika had deposited her generous gift: ham, sausages, a roast, rolls, and pretzels. Had thoroughly cleaned the apartment and vacuumed. She had gone from room to room with a bag in her hand, in search of empty bottles. Behind stacks of books, under the sofa, behind the bench near the curtain, under the desk, behind the wardrobe. Everywhere. Secretly. She was her son's accomplice.

Alcohol, the conductor's baton in our household, directed the tinkling of glass in the full bag. I was defiant. My sense of the theatrical, which I acted out during the day, with the small roles I was paid for and with dancing in the Isadora Duncan School, ended in our sociable nightlife, which I found romantic. I was in love and had no mental distance. I clung to the feelings I was feeling, or to what I wanted for myself. I could not imagine myself without him. It must have been this way, as if I were stuck in this room of love and had lost the key. And just as one eats—yes, without thinking—so had I been caught in the net of Ferdinand's narrative threads, his Cicero lectures, his tireless blarney of justifications, which became an everyday reality through their repetition.

Time is like milk on the stove.

We had two children now. I had given birth to Daniel in the autumn, alone, without Ferdinand, who had slipped off to Mexico months earlier, with a promise we both believed: He would be back before the birth.

The birth. My mother had stayed with Oliver. The doctor concealed his outrage at Ferdinand's absence and mimed the role of father to the newborn Daniel. The birth itself had been easy. We drank champagne and marveled at the babe on my arm.

When I returned home, Oliver lifted my skirt to assure himself that what was lying on my arm as a little bundle was no longer down there.

Happiness anaesthetized my disillusionment with Ferdinand. It had been just the right moment to disappoint my love deeply.

I had Ferdinand's letters as my alibi, could show them to my mother and to my brother, Uli.

On the threshold of a sensational discovery, earthshaking new data...Longing for home, almost drives me insane...

But both of them read more into it, and read between the lines. Above all: lies, and the confirmation of what they had always feared—Ferdinand as meteor, the fireball that ascends and falls, unpreventable, leaving only a vague memory of its credibility. It did not help that I defended him and quarreled with my mother and Uli. Above all, I dared not confess to myself the slightest wavering, any doubt whatsoever.

He quite simply left you alone with two children, Uli said angrily.

My rebellious love leaned against my yearning for bourgeois social order and belonging. Even so, uneasiness crept up my throat like a knot of truth.

What was I to do?

Sell the rug if you need money, or the gold bar, Ferdinand had said when we parted. I actually went off to the Mint with the gold bar, which weighed several pounds.

This is sensational! Such a huge lump of gold! the man said, and disappeared with the gold behind a door. I waited, in my heart the exquisite pleasure of knowing there would soon be thousands of Deutschmarks in my bank account, and waited. Waited. Now I could finally prove to my mother and Uli how deeply he cared for us.

After a long while two gentlemen emerged.

Tja, tja, we are sincerely sorry, you must have looked forward to it so much, but this is just not gold. It is a hoax. Someone has cast various metals together. You need only lick it. One feels the metallic taste right away. Gold is much lighter, and tasteless, they said.

Boy, that would have been lovely for you—and they both laughed in embarrassment.

Three months after Daniel's birth, Ferdinand finally came home. Externally I still stood by him, defended him, permitted no evil word about him. Within me simmered disappointment, deep wounding, rage. It took a long time for me to recover.

During this first phase, love burns a hole in one's consciousness. Happiness is a fetish with which one plays, at one's own discretion, also with the self-evident facility of a juggler. Happiness—so easily brought back with a kiss, blinded by love and the wish for love. Pain—still without its brother, the shared past still so brief, without resonance.

I remember terrible screaming fights. Then old promises were sworn anew, and we made up. The vehemence of the reasons dribbled away into the ridiculous, and my magnanimity, which I so gladly displayed, made me happy. Ferdinand had once again used his charm as a weapon, which had cost him not a bit of effort, merely strengthened him in his vanity.

Love creates an impassible distance between you and the world, and hurls you into the arms of a heavenly illusion.

What bound us together was a sort of complicity against the boredom of the conformist world around us, against mankind, reproducing, earning money, just coasting along in the same old rut—no way did we want to be part of that. But from this point on, a third party lay in wait for us in the citadel. I want to dub him Doubt. Doubt.

•

The room filled with day. Erika had gone. Through the half-open door of Ferdinand's study, ashen mushrooms again squeezed from his pipe. In the vestibule, in the glaring brilliance of a lonely bulb, the bulky oil stove cast a dark shadow, in which all sorts of knickknacks became invisible; along the walls ran bookshelves, which served Oliver as stations when he steamed along the border of the sisal carpet with his wooden train. I stood in the tiny kitchen and cooked. From the vestibule came noises, toot toot, toot toot…choo choo, together with the hum of a bumblebee that bumped irritably against the ceiling. Nestled in a cloth bound at my hips slept Daniel.

Gggrrrr, gggrrrr. Outside, in the tin gutter, a love-crazed pigeon tapped after a lady pigeon. Through the wall broke the uniform tapdance of Ferdinand's typewriter. Tack tack tack tack. Our day, a formless creature in which the hours just sort of ticked along, stood wide open to surprises.

The chime of the doorbell broke shrilly into our idyll.

I'll get it, Mummy, called Oliver, and right away he was back, his eyes wide with excitement.

Mummy, Mummy, a clown is here with his father.

And so it was; I could scarcely bite back my laughter. At the door stood an older gentleman with gray hair and a friendly face, in the company of a woman, a wonderfully colorful creature. A parrot in human form. She had done her face up in the jolliest way: fire-red lips, red cheeks, green eye shadow, red hair in which burned a curved green comb. A large, shrill floral pattern as uniform. Ashley presented us her soft hand, a paw.

Our American visitor was an important man for Ferdinand. Director of a museum, collector of pre-Columbian art, someone who could help him to an unbelievable extent, someone who opened up the vista of a wonderful future. I ran back and forth between kitchen, living room, children's room to take care of the guests. They were speaking English, and I collected small shards of an animated conversation, through which Ferdinand shone like a dancer on a tightrope.

I would like to recall the table where "the clown with his father" sat. The white tablecloth I had brought out because of the importance of the visit, the Meissen setting, upon it the terrine with the hot Bavarian Weisswürste, rolls, mustard and sauerkraut, which I had cooked in white wine, and the company of the thrilled guests. The light of the candles that danced across their expressions, and Ferdinand, the secure sleepwalker with his unbelievable memory for situations, numbers, and exotic names. As he spoke he removed small figurines from his glass case and turned them lovingly into the light. Their shadows danced up the walls and made giants of them. He determined their historical period, described every detail of the places in which they had been found, somewhere in the forest tangle of Mexico. With the sweeping gesture of the prodigy, Ferdinand shaped the history of a small tomb totem into the pulse of the grand Mayan past for the benefit of our guests.

He went on to recount the adventures that led him to this place, who was with him, and, to make it all even more impressive, more seductive, he hauled out heaps of photos. As evidence, he himself stood there, turned toward the camera beneath the huge leafy roof of a tree, next to the rubbing of a stone relief on life-size paper.

A thousand trees will take control of the discovery site, the stone jaguar will be devoured by the confused green, the run of the river will be throttled by the wild applause of the seasons, Ferdinand proclaimed dramatically. I am the ambassador of the gods, who hold their memorial celebration above the pyramids. Their grand history is always threatened by the merciless jungle.

More figurines joined the candles, the crockery, the rest of the table setting on the white linen cloth. A black basalt mask from Teotihuacan, a green serpentine Olmec god, the kneeling form of a man as a vessel, an Olmec face as tomb totem, with a cry on the open lips.

From the floor Oliver provided the conversation with a backdrop of auto-motive sounds.

I was not sitting with them at the table, was running back and forth like a good hostess. I carried little Daniel into the room on my arm to show him around. And Ferdinand was proud of me, of us. We belonged to his collection, to the figurines, the rubbings, the books.

Coatlicue, goddess of love and sin, he called out, and the guests, the clown with his father, lifted their glasses to toast me and the child.

Ferdinand had already packed away his daily quantum of alcohol. He drew near the hour he never noticed; he became unpredictable. Not that he laid hand on anyone: no, more that he no longer had a grip on his passions. At that point he no longer listened to anyone, he monologued, he himself became immense knowledge. In this state, he became an obsessive.

She is insensitive, like an Indio woman, he shrieked. She carries a knife of obsidian at her breast.

Ferdinand danced around me and, as he did so, quoted loudly:

> *Hear, all who are here present,*
> *All who are gathered here,*
> *Yoalliehacatl, "the night wind,"*
> *Has taken pity on us,*
> *For he has laid a gem in the young woman,*
> *The newly married,*
> *A Quetzal feather.*
> *She, the young woman, is pregnant.*
> *He, our Lord,*
> *Has laid in her a child.*

You must be to the house as the heart to the body…you must be as ash and hearth, Ferdinand called out, and the American guests were amused. Perhaps also shocked, slightly irritated, taken aback by the vehemence of the offering. But they played along, they had no choice.

You shouldn't be so stingy—bring more wine. And make coffee, my turtledove.

It was incredibly exhausting. When I replayed his egotistical scenes and cruel outbursts for him, he laughed in my face: You really are just a little petit-bourgeoise.

From outside in the hall I heard Ferdinand's voice, dampened, and, in between, the foreign voices of the guests. Ferdinand urgently needed money, as he wished to take part in excavations. The object of his wooing could fulfill this wish, or so thought Ferdinand. Summon the gods.

And what is the story with these paintings? I heard one of the guests ask.

I could not understand all of it. The coffee machine burbled in between. I waited in the hall, for they were talking about me and my painting, I thought happily. So I waited outside. It must have been a brief exchange, since by the time I went in they were talking about something else.

After a while they had to take their leave, the clown with his father. Ferdinand had pulled out all the stops, shot all his powder.

Thank you, thank you, you're a wonderful cook, they called to me down the corridor.

Midnight had already sounded. I had the baby at my breast. From where I was standing I could still catch a glimpse of Ferdinand, the way he was drawing at his pipe, charmingly helping the lady into her coat; then the three of them vanished from view. They had stepped from the narrow field of the studio a few meters further toward the front door.

Congratulations. In addition to all your other gifts you are a fantastic painter.

The important man patted Ferdinand on the shoulder. I could clearly hear the whole thing. I held my breath. I saw the picture before me, captured as if in a photo.

Oh, that? I just do that on the side.

I heard every tiny sound, the way the three of them pressed through the door, which Ferdinand pulled shut behind him, in order to linger on the landing with the compliment, to suck in the entire praise with the greed of a monster.

Oh, that? I just do that on the side, repeating itself like a scratched disk.

Oh, that? I just do that on the side.

The refrain hung in my ear like a piece of music. My pulse beat the rhythm.

It was my heart that was hammering faster and faster. I could no longer differentiate between pain and rage, was blind with both. My thoughts stammered within me. Tears burned behind my lids. I stared toward the dark door. My throat was knotted up in a scream.

I saw him accompany the guests down the stairs to the street, wait for a taxi with them in front of the entryway. I saw how the cool night wind breezed through his hair, how he moved charmingly, in his best actor's form. I laid Daniel in his bed, went into the kitchen to do the dishes, to think, to order in my mind what actually could not be ordered.

The dishwater ran over my hands, and ran, and ran. I felt horribly lonesome. From the window the night air punched me in the face. Around the hot light bulb at the ceiling, moths circled to their deaths.

The voice of my mother: That one, he thinks only of himself, knows nothing else…

My father: Artist? Make a good match, then you can paint as much as you like. His bitter laugh.

My heart disheveled, empty and full. "She is insensitive. She bears a knife of obsidian at her breast."

At some point I slowly went into the studio on legs I did not know, along the corridor, in which the lonely bulb staged black shadows, on past the wall of books, behind the book façade on which always, always, a squad of empty bottles was piling up, for the accomplice Erika to collect. When one slipped books out they reeked of alcohol, as if they were drunk.

You fucking monster! Rage suppressed my tears, and the knot was still in my throat.

I opened the door. At the table leaned Ferdinand, in the haze of pipe smoke, melted together with the various objects. After the slow-motion act of recognition, he bent over the figures and photos strewn on the table with a broad gesture of his hand, as if to introduce them to me after a long absence.

That one was certainly impressed, he said, pouring himself a glass full and overfull.

He wiped the bespattered photo with his shirtsleeve and hurled back the schnapps in a single gulp.

Aaah, Caramba!

Impressed by you? I asked gravely and pointedly.

Well, yeah….

As he left, you also slipped him the tip that you are the artist around here.

Oh, that—just turned out that way, one word led to another… who gives a shit. He poured himself another one and had to sit down, as he was in danger of toppling over.

Who gives a shit who does the painting around here?

You nasty pig! I scream. I go at him, I have to punch him, punch him in his arrogant grin. I wind up and pummel his head with blow after blow.

He jumps up and lurches away.

A second later a glass streaks through the air and hits my forehead. I let out a shrill cry and fall to the floor. Blood streams across my eyes. I can no longer see.

Later. I sit on the blue sofa, press a towel to the wound on my forehead, to stanch the pulsating blood. Ferdinand has held his head under cold water, to sober up so he can bring me to the doctor. Now he kneels before me on the floor, drenched, and weeping.

Earlier, in the kitchen, I had been beside myself with rage. Angry thoughts had throttled my brain, my heart. And yet now, as he kneels crying before me, I want to take care of him, to avoid feeling my own unbearable pain. I draw him up to me, take him in my arms, his promises murmur sweetly to me, and I believe him, allow myself to be cradled into the illusion of a new, different beginning.

•

We came back from the hospital. In the east, behind the molars of the Alps, waited the day. Through the corridors of the city rolled the sweepers with their carts. In our street the pub door stood wide open to air out last night's stench of cigarettes and alcohol. Chairs stood on the tables, someone swept the floor in the dark interior. Outside the innkeeper leaned squinting toward our taxi. As soon as he recognized Ferdinand, he tapped his forehead in greeting and followed, chased us with his head, as a cat does a bird.

Arriving at our house, Ferdinand and I stomped up the stairs, closely intertwined. Four flights. By the second floor Ferdinand's arm had slipped from our sweet entanglement.

From here you can make it back up by yourself, darling. I'm going to quickly grab a newspaper.

It's still too early, I said confusedly, still much too early.

I held a gauze bandage to my forehead, which was still numb from the local anesthetic.

Oh, I'll find one, he called out, bounding off down the stairs, quickly, nimbly. Two steps at once, with the elasticity of a beast after its prey.

Down on the street he will turn left, cross the intersection in one leap. The innkeeper in the doorway will give himself a light shove, push off from the wall, as if someone had tapped him, go behind the counter, take two glasses from the drying rack, and pour two Grappas.

Morning, says Ferdinand, sits on the barstool, takes the glass. Cheers! Whoosh, he tips it down his throat. Aaaaahh, he says, clenches his teeth, draws the air through, and grins.

So, what brings you out so early? asks the innkeeper, who knows everything and has to know everything, know it for his guests, since otherwise he would not be a good, beloved innkeeper. Certainly, that's how he makes his living in the end.

Oh, my wife ran into an open window last night, so mindless. She gave herself a deep cut.

Oh, God, that's stupid, says the innkeeper.

Yes, five stitches.

Oh well, it'll heal up.

I told her the same thing. No one will notice in a few weeks. She can hold on to her beauty, he said as a kind of Machiavellian footnote.

I looked at my scar in the mirror and could not help bursting out in tears. Another scar I had thought long since healed now stared at me once again.

"Well—an artiste!?" says my father. Subtext: Artist? You would like to become an artist? Like your lazy grandfather? Meaning Max, my mother's father, who did not have to work and painted wonderfully.

Marry. Make a good match, then you can paint as much as you like.

It wounds me, his bitter laughter above all. He does not even bother to look at what I have drawn.

The scar is red and thick, held together with four threads. I gently stroke it. It will be a few weeks before the pink line starts to dissolve, becomes a thin white millimeter.

I can call my father's bitter laughter to mind at will, like a reel of film, a curse that lingers. Am I good? I ask myself.

Despite his recognition of me as a person, I was not praised for my painting, not by my father.

I lie on the bed and weep until morning dawns, I have to get up, take care of Oliver and Daniel.

Have I made a good match? And at some point I hear the key in the door. Ferdinand is back, with the paper.

•

The thing I know: we reconciled again and again. He cried easily, perhaps over a love scene in a book. Perhaps it reminded him of something profoundly his own. Perhaps he was part of a collective sadness.

I remember my father telling him how he had helped his Jewish friends, never hesitating for a moment. My father spoke quite calmly: Hitler was the greatest criminal. And Ferdinand cried. My feelings for him were strong and forgiving in those days, like a mother's for her child.

I drafted a list with the good aspects of our marriage opposite the bad, and I imagined my strength could be his salvation. I saw his true face. Seldom, but altogether clearly. Saw a deep pain behind the curtain of his stage appearances. Compared with it my own sorrows spelled themselves out as a bagatelle.

Smoky Language of the Wind

WHEN I STOOD BY OUR STUDIO WINDOW, I looked out over a sea of red tiled roofs, with the church tower, whose bell kept the time, opposite at catty-corners. When I leaned out, I could see the street below winding like a river between the rows of houses.

Not too much traffic. Occasionally a child jumped after its ball. A mutt ran busily down the pavement, came to a stop, sniffed, lifted its leg at the fence. A woman lugged a full shopping bag.

Early in the morning a delivery van curved into the picture, swung into its parking place in front of the bakery; a man with a delivery cap on his head climbed out, cranked open the rear door, nimbly sprang up the three steps to the shop, went in, only to reappear immediately, carrying with both hands a basket piled high with loaves of bread. He cautiously probed his way down the steps, stowed away his burden in the van, banged the door shut, swung himself up into the driver's seat, and whizzed off.

On the façade across the street lay the glaring sun. As soon as someone on the corresponding floor of the house opposite pushed open a window, a steel knife of light slit through our studio and remained stuck at the door. The sharp slice of light made me attentive; I looked up from my easel, and sometimes the lovely Mrs. Warburg stood there on the balcony opposite. She had reputedly "sowed up" her husband's career, to use the drastic Bavarian expression. Yes, sowed it right up. Her husband, a diplomat, had been called to Washington as ambassador. At one of the embassy parties a journalist asked, how was she settling in here in the city?

Not at all, she answered scornfully.

So, have you already made friends with the wives of the other diplomats? the unruffled journalist drilled deeper.

No.

Do you like it here with us in the U.S.A.?

I find everything dreadful here, including your stupid questions.

Sometimes she bent over the banister of the balcony. Her long, rust-red hair, which gave a glow to her white porcelain face, fell across her shoulders onto her bosom. For some minutes she would stand motionless, observing something down there on the street, with the fullest attention. I could not see the scene that so fascinated her that she seemed frozen into salt, like Lot's wife. Only a little breeze played with her hair, with the collar of her blouse.

No matter how far I stretched forward, leaned out from the tiny sub-window in the midst of the many small squares that made up the studio window— the only part one could open—the roof and the gutter blocked my view of the street below.

I knew the watering hole, the fur shop, and our entrance. Whatever was holding the lovely Mrs. Warburg transfixed must have been played out down there in a dead corner, whose enigma became more and more of an idée fixe.

And at rare intervals I saw Mr. Warburg, the former diplomat, standing on the balcony. A child sucking its thumb, he pulled impotently on a cigar that refused to draw properly. He turned to face the wall, lowered his head between his shoulders, formed a room with his hands, flared up a match, and puff, puff, little clouds of smoke hopped through his fingers.

He did not look down onto the street. His sole preoccupation was the cigar; the gestures of the lighting-up ritual repeated themselves several times before he took the cold cigar from his mouth, held it between thumb and forefinger right in front of his eyes, like something incomprehensible, foreign. With an irritated mien he cast a fleeting glimpse at the sky, contemptuously stubbed out the cigar butt in one of the flowerpots that decorated the balcony, turned, and finally disappeared back through the door into his apartment.

Did the Warburgs register who was visiting the watering-hole?

Beneath their balcony the tips of a chestnut tree grew green. In May the green buds would conjure forth wonderful blossom candles. The buzzing of the bees, as they went about their honey business, flew all the way over to me. Later, when the blossoms began to wither, the millions of little flakes that had been whirled away by the upcurrent collected in our gutter.

But what was playing itself out down on the street? What was kept from me while I guarded the citadel above?

As soon as Ferdinand got ready to leave our apartment, something tense in his bearing melted away. Even at the door, out on the landing, some force, some alienating tractor beam, seemed to lure him. I gave a last wave down the stairway; he waved back up. His step morphed into agile leaps. I could still see his mane of hair, his back, then the dark staircase swallowed him up. None of the windows allowed me to see in what direction he had vanished.

This fact, at root quite unimportant, drilled away at my curiosity. I wanted to know more. Too much mystery was lounging around Ferdinand. It gnawed away like the teeth of a marten, behind the studio wall—the craving for news—greedy and new, vulnerable. I counted the bottles that he emptied every evening, guests or no, counted the Underbergs—the alcoholic digestive bitters he pronounced the supreme good and was knocking back one after the next. 16 to 25 a day; I found them in places that for me were no longer hiding-places. Books slid forward on the shelves. My sharpened eye immediately saw the bags in the corners under the sofa, like freshly dug mounds that betray the lair of a fox.

I swayed between anger and concern. I was angry when he promised to rein in the drinking but left it at empty words. Sober, I could reach him, but only when the two of us were alone. Scarcely had the guests arrived when he succeeded in degrading me to a narrow-minded petty bourgeoise who simply did not understand the soul of a real man. Too young and inexperienced.

Then, once again, Ferdinand recited for me with all his charm and pathos. In the background breathed a pan flute of longing prophecies, in the smoky language of the wind.

> *From the land of the rain*
> *And the fog*
> *I come,*
> *Xochiquetzal,*
> *To the land of putrefaction*
> *I must go.*

He staged it all so perfectly that I would burst out laughing. This was often the beginning of joyful hours where my love for Ferdinand found its meaning again, where the gods and their mythology bewitched me once again, where I listened to the precision of the mystical names with fascination. Tecpancaltzin, the eighth king of the Toltecs. Papanzin, the prince. The beautiful Xochitl. The ancient goddess Ilamatecuhtli. Chicomeocôatl, the goddess of corn. Cintéotl, the god of corn. Goddess Uuixtociuatl. Goddess Xochiquetzal. Xochipilli, her twin brother.

Briefly I shared his passion. My curiosity had a rest. I waited again for what there was no answer for. We would pack the children into the car and drive out to the edge of town, to our Schrebergarten. For a few hours we would play with hope.

But before long, it would rebel once again within me.

Where are you hurrying off to now? I wanted to know.

I need to get some fresh air, he would say.

He felt himself imprisoned in the cage of bourgeois normalcy and longed for the companionship of those "real men." He had to go there. He had to scratch an itch. There, where he had first caught the corner of my eye, at Sausage Resi's vegetable stand, under her alcoholic parasol, before I really knew him. He had to hurry back there, at least for a few hours, into the world so familiar to him.

Ferdinand had been forced to close The Hot Club. Too few people were still interested in jazz. Rock-and-roll and pop had conquered the young. Ferdinand found the new rhythms beneath discussion and boycotted my interest in seeing the Beatles play Munich, even though everyone was wild about them. He resisted it with the vehemence of a wrestler in a match, as if he feared something in this new phenomenon or had to prove something. In our atelier mariachi music pounded through the days.

It seemed he had to defend our world, the familiar, keep me imprisoned in it. He was suddenly unmoored. He stood in the middle of the room, candlelight caressed him, and I could feel his helplessness, his fear of losing me. Lose me to the Beatles? He was basically afraid of this new society—one reason more to drink, knock something back.

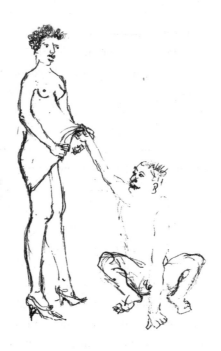

I think it was then that I began to grow up. I lost my innocence and probed about in an unknown alphabet, seeking to redefine myself. It was no longer just about Ferdinand. I was no longer just a figurine from his collection. Even my handwriting grew larger, clearer, more definite.

I stole the time to paint. Into the studio streamed northern light, cool and shadowless. At the window stood my children's playpen, in which I had set up my easel, next to it a round metal table, on which a piece of marble served as a palette. Oil colors, brushes, turpentine, painter's oil, and, amidst all these utensils, in the middle, the ball of stone.

I stood before the white canvas. The first, still-hesitant stroke of color was followed by one more decisive, courageous, and I felt how by lighting a small candle I was igniting a glorious crystal chandelier, felt how a thousand facets began to dance, how one thought took on the form of a whole picture. I pushed fear aside. Once again I was happy.

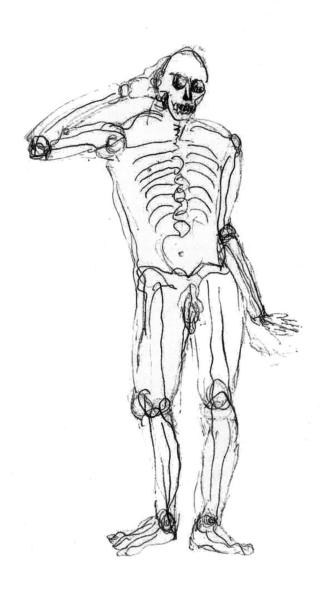

Part Three

Heart, be brave, if you cannot bear grief, go—
Love's glory is not a small thing,
Come in, if you are fearless,
Shudder, and this is not your house.

—Rumi

The Journey

ON THE HORIZON, behind the precise silhouettes of the houses, a fire-red pencil counted the last minutes of the day. An impatient ice moon already hung in the sky. The long silver tail of the train, in which we had just stowed away our luggage, awaited its departure.

Ferdinand and I traveled first to Bremerhaven, then further, with a freighter, to Mexico. Our five-year-old, Oliver, was with us. A few friends had gathered on the platform in the central Munich station to wish us farewell; my mother, too, of course, my brother, and his wife Lo. Lo held the hand of our little Daniel, who was to spend the next three months, the length of the journey, in her house with her five sons.

I pressed Daniel firmly to me, until I had to let him go, my little talisman, from whom I did not wish to part, yet had to. He was, after all, only two years old.

A long journey, hard to predict. And dangerous, perhaps. This journey was to initiate me into Ferdinand's pre-Columbian world and make me his excited consort. From the outside the scene here in the station looked like an ordinary, cheery farewell. But for me it meant venturing into a new, unknown, also hopeful phase of my life. Breaking open something that had been closed to me until now.

Everything that interrupts the banality of everyday life bears the secret of renewal and the birth of an illusion.

With a bang the cork slipped out of the champagne bottle. Uli poured everyone a paper cupful. We had to toast one another quickly, before the conductor blew the whistle. Ferdinand lifted the window in our compartment.

Bye-bye, bye-bye, bon voyage, come back in one piece.

We waved, held Oliver out over the edge of the window. Bon voyage, good luck. We were already moving forward. I still saw Daniel sitting upon Uli's shoulders, both his little arms in the air. Thrilled by the train and the station, he had not really grasped the implications of our goodbye. I cried, then lost sight of the diminutive figure on Uli's shoulders. The train, gathering speed, was already falling into the rhythm of its heartbeat. White handkerchief doves fluttered above the group of toy people.

Velocity carried us forth, united our bodies, our thoughts. Encased in the silver hull, the waking and the dreamers raced through the nightly ceremony of buildings, interwoven streets, indigo woods, repeated in the mirror of the windowpanes, the drowsy rhythm of the northward-rushing train.

Again and again, as we approached some little town, the long, warning whistle tooted through the night, across the frame of the train, fusion of steel and air. The iron horse shot through the station with undiminished speed, dissolved the bodies of the waiting passengers into faceless daubs of color, only to gather in the wide night-blue land once more as soon as it passed the ornamental bastion of architecture.

•

One could read by the light of the moon.

One evening Bobsi Orentschuck had turned up at our place. Bobsi—my much older admirer, whom I had not seen for years, the one who had given me the white leather coat with black fur. He had to check on how we were doing, how I was doing. He wanted to meet my husband, about whom he had heard so much, since his business dealings often brought him to Mexico.

In our atelier, a colorful mix of friends and strangers were jumbling about.

We have friends in common in Mexico City who have told me about your legendary Ferdinand, Bobsi laughed.

He drew me aside. He was no taller than I, speaking right into my ear. It had been eight years for sure since we had seen one another. But distance and time had not weakened his interest in me.

How are you doing? Do you still have the black-and-white dog? he lisped.

Yes, he's asleep somewhere around here. He is as old now as that coat I still have from you, I said with a laugh.

Really? It's been eight years. You still have that coat? You've become a grown woman.

Of course I still had the coat. Never in a million years could I afford such a piece of luxury. And I said:

What do you think? I wear it to this day.

And Bobsi beamed. The coat was a piece of himself, a symbol, and it had been simpler for me to love the gift than the giver.

Yes, while Ferdinand served up his stories, realities, illusion, disillusion, dreams, Bobsi became the deerstalker, to sound out the terrain pregnant with *mysterium*.

He strode through our apartment, opened the oriel window in our bedroom. A car horn blared out. The squeaking of brakes pressed up over the gutter into the apartment. For a reflective moment, he stood next to the stove colossus in the corridor. His gaze rode along the bookshelves, up to the gash in the wallpaper. He pushed open the bathroom door.

Above the tub, hung out to dry, fastened with clothespins, were Ferdinand's black-and-white photographic studies: Usumacinta near Yaxchilán, Indian children in the jungle, Lacandonians on the Rio Lacanuja, Indios in front of a baroque church, market day in Chamoula. The images still clung tightly to the secret Mexico. He nodded with a smile and studied every one.

While I sang Oliver and Daniel their lullaby, Bobsi sat with us, stroked the boys' heads. Sweet dreams, he said.

In the tiny kitchen, water was boiling for spaghetti. Miniature cars were parked next to the stove on the linoleum diamond floor. The electric water heater hissed. There was scarcely room for two. Bobsi pushed past me on the pretense of checking out the view of the apartment across the way. And as if by accident he held me for a moment, my back firmly pressed against him, and kissed my hair, my neck.

Laughter wafted across from the studio, wind whispers of an Andean pan flute; the old faun Bobsi stood grinning in the doorway. I handed him the wooden spoon.

You stir the spaghetti, I said.

Fat sizzled in the pan; the garlic cloves began to dance. I threw in onions and ground beef. Thyme, basil, salt and pepper. Tomato paste.

In the atelier Ferdinand was doing his cooking with magic. He was giving a lecture. His words danced over to us through the vestibule in intermittent scraps.

The goddess Coatlicue, who cries in her serpent dress. Only human blood can calm her…Four destroyed Aztec worlds…Human hearts, human blood appease her…Hurtling into the abyss…The monstrous earthquake rips the five suns down with it into the great darkness…a kind of atomic destruction…A prophecy for our time, Ferdinand called out and drew at his pipe. I heard the click-clack of his teeth on its mouthpiece…Mankind must sacrifice its most exquisite possessions to the gods.

Bobsi stirred the steaming pot of spaghetti. I roasted the Bolognese.

…Human blood. Human hearts are to maintain the strength of the gods, preserve mankind from its downfall.

Cheers, called Ferdinand.

Fascinating, someone said.

Dreadful, so cruel: a woman's voice.

Wouldn't you like to visit me in Mexico one of these days? Bobsi asked, handing me the bowl so that I could mix the meat sauce into the pasta.

It'd be great, I said gamely. But for Ferdinand and me both to take a trip like that is just not in the cards financially.

Bobsi smiled.

A stone axe with the head of an ape grinned between the plates on the table. A mask of slime-green jade stared at us in astonishment. I shoved them both aside to make room for the bowl of spaghetti. But Ferdinand's hand reached nimbly in and carried off the objects lovingly, indeed tenderly, putting them back into the cupboard where he stored his special treasures.

Bobsi had put on an apron and played chef, played bohemian. Ferdinand praised his cooking. We feasted and chattered and toasted one another.

On his pass through my multifaceted world, Bobsi had quickly drawn himself a sketch. And, true to this type of successful man, he wanted to add color to the sketch and impress me. Amidst this emotional complexity, hidden, yet manifest, irritatingly oblique, as vehemently near as it is coolly distanced, calculated, he wanted to lay his trump card on the table.

He stood up, raised his glass, tapped his fork on its rim. The clatter of the cutlery on the plates died away. Our friends' conversations and thoughts stood still. Everyone was watching Bobsi.

I hereby invite my dear friends Ferdinand and Beatrix on a three-month trip to Mexico. You will be my guests, you needn't worry about anything. Everything included.

For a moment it was quite still, as if in a hallucination, making our confused minds reorder normal thought patterns, delaying the perception of what they had just heard.

All the noise now, the laughter, hearty pats on the shoulder, toasts, the grin of recognition.

Noble, fantastic, magnificent, magnanimous!

All of which resounded in Bobsi's ears like the finale to a great overture. Bobsi, our friend, our patron—for in our world there were only poor devils and dreamers.

As so often, to eke out time for his reactions, Ferdinand was busy with his pipe. He grinned all the while, did not wish to appear too thrilled, since Bobsi had suddenly stolen the stage and ambushed him. Ferdinand rummaged for words, and slowly, after the pipe was cleaned, freshly packed, was steaming once again, he slipped over to Bobsi and tapped him on the shoulder.

Bobsi, smart investment. You really did it right this time, he said boldly.

Coincidental meetings take place unpredictably, the way beasts encounter one another at night. We tread magical, precisely drawn paths toward one another, blindfolded.

One of Bobsi O's businesses exported printing machines to South America. Our trip began in Bremerhafen, and brought us to Mexico on a freighter. Thus we found ourselves, Ferdinand, Oliver, and I, in the company of a handful of other adventurers with similar hopes, similar reasons: the love of travel, or the need to get to the other continent.

Like the tone from a tuba, memory rises up gently at first, then more sharply. White fishbone clouds in the May sky above. Far beyond, at the horizon, a ribbon of dark azure surrounded us, not land, not the end of a beginning.

Millions of silvery prisms danced their wedding high in the atmosphere. Heavy mingled with light, water with air.

The freighter seemed to be pitching in the unfathomable darkness like a paper boat gone astray. But when one stood up in the bow, amidst the whirling sea cocktail of salt and mint, one felt how the energy of the ship struggled against the power of the sea, pressed forward against the violence of the elements with the potency of invention.

The little paper ship, symbolizing a completely incomprehensible loneliness round about us, accompanied me on this wondrous journey. I stood on the deck; a kerchief wound round my head restrained my hair against the capricious breeze that blew my skirt up into a balloon and almost carried me off with it.

We scarcely saw Oliver, who was always off playing with the sailors down in the belly of the beast. They loved the novelty of having a child on board.

A guest sat in the windbreak of the captain's quarters and read. Another lay sunning himself in the nest of a rolled-up rope. Through the window I saw Ferdinand chatting with the captain. They seemed intimate, like old confidantes. While they talked, the captain's fleshy red paw fell in brotherly confidentiality upon Ferdinand's shoulder. Compared with him Ferdinand was almost dainty. He looked up at the captain and rested his handsome be-ringed hand on his arm.

Observing this physical familiarity, I recalled earlier, similar scenes with other men who ranked themselves "real men." The same gestures, the same tilt of the head, the same friendly fraternal taps, the same smile, pipe in mouth. The grin of agreement, needing no further words. The feints.

The captain and Ferdinand could not see me, on account of the bright sunlight. Or they did not notice me, were too busy with their ceremony of recognition, with their laughing amazement at their fraternal resemblance. I gave a sharper look and thought: they really do look similar, in profile, in the mirror of the windowpane, against the monotonous hard color outside, where I stand with my skirt as my sail.

Each held a glass in his hand, toasted the other, drank, grimaced, squinted, while the pungent elixir glided down their gullets. Saufbrüder.

Cool air brushed my brow there in the shade. The metal of the railing I was holding onto was cool. Like an official, I registered what happened, held on decorously to it, drew it up, counted it. Through the glass windowpane I could not hear the words. But I saw the fascination that they triggered, mirrored in the face of the stocky figure in a captain's uniform. And I saw myself there, in the glass, swept away by the storyteller's art, and could not bring myself to climb the stairs, open the door and—what?

My mother's warnings and Uli's dismissive remarks about Ferdinand's character had long since fallen silent. My benevolent family switched to generalities, to helpless lies of acceptance. Old warnings do not stay fresh.

There was no real drinking in my family. Now and then one enjoyed wine—a cigar, likewise—but in moderation. I knew nothing of excess, still less of the consequences. No one actually knew a character like Ferdinand. Perhaps as a fascinating story, away from us, yes, that for sure, a figure in a novel, someone to discuss, to shake one's head over in wonder, making a little noise of contempt. But not so close to home. Heavens, no, one's own daughter!

The captain, solitary, at home here on the freighter, in his element, acted as center of gravity to a group of types who, thrown together in leisure by necessity, quickly and effortlessly found their way to a common attitude. Inside the berth, whiskey, schnapps, card games, trumped by fantastic tales, stranger-ly friends outbid one another in importance, traceless travelers rolled together in the wastes of the Atlantic.

I did not go up the stairs to Ferdinand, nor did I open the door. A sick feeling crept up within me, from my stomach, or from my heart. I could not think the simplest thought. I turned away from what was causing me pain and helplessness at the same time. I turned, went slowly along the rolling monstrosity to the rear deck, and leaned over the balustrade. Below me, heaped up in the belly of the ship, wedged together, the freight lined up and piled up: crates concealing

machine parts, lashed down with metallic bands. Further out, the rolling black water sucked the white foam down with it.

And amidst the monotonous noise I felt a deadly stillness. Within me there whispered, crept up, a cold premonition, the opposite of the fascination one feels for a human being, the one that mixes so sweetly and compliantly with the elixir Love, and, for a certain while, turns you blind, deaf, dumb.

The partings in my childhood flashed by, first loves that innocently, it is said, yet deeply, unforgettably, primally imprint themselves. Back then, I realized for the first time that there are always new loves, others.

I gave a start. I had not heard him coming, on account of the loud racket that surrounded me. Ferdinand pressed me to him, bound me fast, as if with a rope. Was it to be near me, or was it to stabilize himself, to bring the ship's pitching and tossing into unison with his own? I would all too willingly have snuggled up to him. I still loved him so much. I smelled the schnapps on his breath. I felt his arm on my shoulder, but at the same time a different, stronger arm held me: my thoughts.

I do not remember any storm on this voyage, only a chronic nausea climbing up from my stomach. Bitter, uncontrollable, like thoughts.

In the evening, when violet melted the sea together with the sky, the stars clambered one after the other from the atmosphere, first tender, then more pronouncedly and clearly: the Milky Way, strewing the nightly firmament with sugar of magic. The nights annihilated our existence on the freighter to a tiny glowworm at the extreme tip of the world. The capricious steel steed rode on, delicately enfolded in a shell of moody crystal air, galloped through plankton, pushed through billions of fish, sea-serpents, coral skeletons—imagination, slashed into facets by the frosty moon, will-o'-the-wisp of familiar contours, arbitrary coastlines.

Ciudad de México

FINALLY FIRM GROUND BENEATH ONE'S FEET AGAIN. Glad for our arrival, the civilized, urbane wildness of Ciudad de México embraced us. Bewitched by Bobsi's world of luxury, gatherings that went till dawn, mariachi musicians that followed us with their songs all the way into the house where we lived. A never-ending party we danced through.

Ferdinand was effusive: Mexico, a country that was so proud of its artists, that supported them so willingly, whose cultural conscience allowed them to conjure up gigantic frescoes on the walls of houses. Yes, even on the cliff walls along the highway the traveler was accompanied by the political symbols of an egalitarian future.

> *We condemn so-called easel painting, and all the art produced by*
> *ultra-intellectual circles on the grounds that it is aristocratic, and*
> *we glorify the expression of monumental art because it is publics'*
> *[sic] property.*

> *Art must be accessible to all, and every artist must contribute to*
> *the glorification of the energy of the masses, and to the goal of an*
> *egalitarian future.*

Diego Rivera, José Orozco, and David Sequeiros were called Los Tres Grandes. The circle of frescoes and monument painters extended itself still further. There was Roberto Montenegro, Rufino Tamayo, Jorge González Camarena, Desiderio Hernández Xochitiotzin and Petro Nel Gómez. It was fantastic. Juan

O'Gorman personally showed us his frescoes on the history of Mexico, in Castle Chapultepec. He introduced us to their historical personages: Cŭaŭhtémoc, Moctezuma, Hernán Cortés, Miguel Hidalgo, José Maria Morelos y Pavón, Porfirio Diaz, Emiliano Zapata, Francisco Villa, whose names were so familiar to me, heroes of song and story, passionately sung in the revolutionary ballads which rang through the days in our Munich atelier.

I loved the ease of our lives then in Mexico City. Ferdinand was the *hombre muy guapo, muy brilliante*, with his beautiful wife, the painter, with the lovely child. In the suburb of San Angel Inn, spectacular colonial villas opened their gates. Indios stepped a few paces back and shyly lowered their heads. Through the tropical green gardens shimmered the flower-dress scraps of their children and wives, who lived in the interior along the walls and watched over the great villas from the shadows of their abodes. There, a miniature settlement crouched at a silent distance. There, behind twig fences, beneath tin roofs, mats made of palm leaves, lived the gardeners, the cooks, the raisers of chickens. Sometimes one heard a song of pain and of joy. Quarrelsome shouting. Shrill barking of dogs. A martin ran tiptoe across glass shards that crowned the wall.

Juan O'Gorman, artist and architect, had built half his house into a cliff. Audacious architecture played hide-and-seek with exotic nature. Like his exquisitely painted surreal pictures, it was closely bound up with the unrestrained genius of the tropical garden. Above the dinner table hung, like a gigantic, lightless chandelier, a moss-covered rock on which lizards slithered about. Little clumps of earth, green fibers, fell on our tableware, into the tamale bowls, on gazpacho, mixed themselves into the guacamole. The exotic setting was accompanied by the twittering of birds and the rasping of parrots. When one looked carefully, there were sleeping geckoes, pale blue, on the blue wall up the stairs leading to the bedrooms.

Juan O'Gorman, tall, slender, reserved but friendly. He looked at the works I had brought along and surprised me, the young, completely unknown artist,

with an invitation to take part in a group exhibition. I would never have allowed myself to dream of such a thing.

You paint like the Surrealists, like Max Ernst, Magritte, I see you up there with myself, he said with a smile.

And Goya, I asked, my favorite painter?

Yes, him too, perhaps, he said.

I was overjoyed. Juan O'Gorman had peered into my soul.

A circle of friends, refugees, artists from all over the world, had found its way here. And Mother Mexico had embraced them.

In the domicile of Dr. Kurt Stafenhagen, there hung a collection of contemporary pictures, next to several Rivera paintings, among them the portrait of Mrs. Stafenhagen. Abstract compositions by Matta and the psychological pictures of Remedios Varo, who had fled the Nazis with the poet Péret. They all went to and fro in this house. Here they were all collected and supported, here they left behind their gentle and their unrestrained gestures, and here, amidst all the rich treasures, I encountered Frida Kahlo.

My first overwhelming impression. It hit me back then like a powerful impact, a kind of epistemological shock, paired with the feeling of spiritual affinity. I could not tear my eyes away. Amidst all the treasures on the wall I read into her history. I grasped her symbols. Sun with leaf. Frida Kahlo painted biography—exotic, alien, and, at the same time, cruelly close at hand: the androgynous glance, shadowed by swallow's-wing brows, the eyes of a child. Primal fragility, dignified and ancient like Mexican history. Narcissus, she held in her hand the mirror in which I recognized my own self.

The Stafenhagens, close friends to Diego and Frida and the whole clique of artists, filled us with quite different, private stories, offbeat and scandalous. The gigantic Rivera, with his unrestrained appetite for sex and admiration, pulled all women into bed with him. The decorative Frida countered with her own sexual escapades. Jealousy, conquest, lovers. and mistresses separated the two of them and brought them back together again.

That Frida and Trotsky worked side by side to create the Mexican communist movement has passed into the history books. And yet Fridita, as her friends called her, was saucy and courageous. At a party she is said to have written on her bare rear end: I am a F.W. (I am a Fucking Wonder).

Ferdinand listened politely, for during this period he was very gregarious. But then he demonstrated his contempt by moving to a more serious theme, turned away from our illustrious conversation, picked up a book and fled into his pre-Columbian world. Ferdinand was afraid of Frida, of her example, of her independence, her personality, her sexuality. Fear of what impression she would make on me with her testament to truth. For women, whom he often denoted as "broads," Ferdinand had thought out a tidy moral corset, into which he liked to wedge them.

An hysteric—I cannot abide hysterical women, he puffed when we were alone again, and, as if accidentally, bumped a full glass off the table onto the stone floor. *Krrrr peng.*

But I had already run laughing out the door, to the waiting car of Mrs. Stafenhagen, who was taking me along to Coyoacán, an old quarter of México-Ciudad, to the Casa Azul, Frida's house.

A while driving. We talked about Frida's headstrong fashions, her style, her dainty beauty. And Mrs. Stafenhagen compared me with Frida. I too am dressed in a very headstrong, very conspicuous way, with a courageousness and loudness that are similar to Frida's. Oh, how I vacuumed up her words. She was a kind woman, but she sometimes judged people with a sharply critical and skeptical eye. Hence the compliment felt particularly sweet.

And already we saw it: the azure-blue walls that embraced the villa.

We entered the house. It seemed occupied, as if Frida had left it only for a short time. Her pictures and drawings were a diary of her miscarriages; of her bloody, frequent operations,; of sex. On the easel stood a self-portrait with a little monkey on her shoulder. Her white, lacy clothes, which transformed her into the Woman of Tehuana, hung in wardrobes. Open doors, other intimate paintings, Frida's jewelry, ribbons, blossoms. Her skivvies. Her corsets. The crutches. The shoes. I was the voyeur, initiated by a queen into the inmost ritual. Next to her bed waited Diego's gigantic shoes, like a reliquary that demonstrated that he was at home here after all. She had catalogued her life exactly, in the certainty of becoming a legend. Self-dramatization as an art form.

I saw in this blue house the gloved hand of love, which holds fast to what cannot be explained, tender and brutal.

Yes, in the Ciudad de México of this time, which for all of us was filled with everything new, including the calm required for leisure; in the colorful cadence of foreign languages; in the gardens that fenced in the villas of our hosts—in all of it was an opportunity for a deep catching of one's breath. Ferdinand was mirrored in the admiration of our friends—fellow foreigners who, in the coziness of pecuniary stability, indulged in the pleasure of art and the art of living. And the admiration contributed to his feeling of being uplifted, as if by some higher source.

Yes, during this time, perhaps protected by the affluence of our host Bobsi and his friends, for a brief moment, Ferdinand was as he once had been, back when I first got to know him: he was glad, in love with the music of his own stories, without the self-righteous philosophizing of the alcoholic. He had listeners; their history was his element. The clouds between us had opened up; a fan of sunrays slipped through, as if in a medieval painting.

I see Ferdinand before me, as he contemplates himself in a convex mirror. Only in the middle can the accurate portrait be seen, and only for as long as one remains absolutely still and does not give in to the temptation to move the picture and thus distort it.

Yo creo que es él

STRANGENESS IN A STRANGE LAND. Neither the rooms nor the stairs in a house where one has lived, imprinted on one's memory like lines on one's hand. No, strange, every moment pursued by another, captured as if in a photograph, tiny, fleeting facets that join up, yet always leave gaps. Scents without history. The song of nature remains a riddle. The foreign language makes you a modest beggar.

After the superb time in the Ciudad de México, when I was so unexpectedly celebrated as a painter, a present from the gods—there, where I found Ferdinand again, was happy, dared hope, where the phantoms that held him in thrall had fled into the obscure past—from there we set out on our journey southward. But in the unpredictable, enigmatic succession of events that makes up our lives, what I had forgotten, what I did not want to think about, repeated itself again and again. As the city let go of us, the old beast crept back, until Ferdinand understood his own existence only in the fraternal embrace of alcohol.

Our goal was to arrive at the Yucatán jungle, at the sites of the ruins I knew well from photographs. Except that now I was to smell the ruins, taste them, hear their Lorelei song, to understand Ferdinand totally.

There is a beautiful place, the city of Cuernavaca, with a superb climate, situated higher up above the seabed on which the Ciudad de México was built. It is cooler up there. There the rich have their summer villas. Around the swimming pools, magenta walls of bougainvillea and beds of oleander sun themselves. Beneath rosy archways, white peacocks drag their bridal trains across mats of grass. Other birds, incandescent green, with yellow beaks, sail shrieking over the high walls, down into the neighboring gardens. Immediately adjacent, in symbiotic dependency, live the Indio communes of domestic spirits, with the *kikeriki*

of roosters, clucking of hens, barking of dogs. From there the sweet smell of cooked corn wafts across.

Finding a black-and-white snapshot from Mexico brings me back to that journey so long ago. In the photo, Bobsi O, little Oliver, a young man, and I are walking along a country road. On the back is written: On the way to the temple of Tlaloc Huitzilopochtli. We are on the way to the pyramid Teopanzolco... As yet there is no tourism such as would come along later. Only a few travelers, curiosity-seekers, addicts, refugees from far away. Ourselves. Bobsi O. and the expatriates, who love Mexico with hearts full of virginal humanity and longing.

On the way to this pyramid... rural dirt road, white baroque church. We rounded the Plaza Municipal, chestnut trees dozed around a dried-up fountain. Perching on stone benches, in the shadows, were men tired since the day they were born; thoughts too deep for words wintered in their eyes. Domino tables with black-and-white checkered patterns awaited the game. The midday heat bound everything to the plaza. Even the birds hid in the dust-green hedges. With a gentle rustling, tired leaves released themselves from the day and landed silently on the hard-trampled earth.

We left the sleepy plaza and found ourselves back on the street in the photo. Suddenly we saw, just a few meters away, a man lying there before us, his arms outstretched as if on Goya's crucifixion painting.

Don't make any false moves, whispered Bobsi. We simply go on past the man. Act as if you don't see him. Look in the other direction.

Birds of prey were circling slowly and deliberately above. There was a fragile stillness all about, as if in a glass prison. Not a soul to be seen. The doors, the windows—faceless. The man lay there as if dead: his breast in the open dirty-white shirt was smeared with blood, stubble blackened his face, flies sat on the red wound.

Oliver, look over there, behind the trees. You can see something moving.

We had to distract him. He was always so curious and free. Let the man sleep, we said.

We moved on, anxiously blabbering something or other among ourselves, and quickly left the scene behind. We were never to find out what really happened. On the way back we found that the body had disappeared without a trace. The street wound rust-red through the green disorder. A few Indios squatted on the shoulder.

Buenos días, they said, answering our greeting.

Later in our journey we were to meet up with a "dead man" several more times. A bloody bundle of child was part of the scenario staged here for us and other gringos, so that we would stop to help, show ourselves compassionate.

We would recount these bloody encounters as an amusement, but also as a warning, for behind them was a wicked prank: under certain circumstances you yourself could be the dead person, robbed on account of your compassion. Behind the silent fences, the dead windows, the black doors, in the bushes, lurked desperadoes.

•

Cuernavaca. Ferdinand had already been here on earlier trips. Colonial villas and baroque churches line the streets. There stands the palace of Cortés, built in 1533 above the Teocali. Ruins of old sugar-cane factories. Sapodilla trees ringed the marketplace, where one could find anything; it sticks in my memory like an alchemist's lair.

Oliver had a fever, as children easily do when traveling. Remembering the natural medicines my mother had treated me with as a child, the three of us went to the marketplace.

An Indian woman as old as the trees x-rayed my feverish little Oliver with her yellow eyes, in order to treat him with the dried treasures of plants, tendons, flowers, mushrooms, and elements of animal carcasses; all this curious assortment more reminiscent of death than of life.

She picked and chose, she murmured gently to herself, she chewed betel nut, orange-red juice between her stone teeth. First she nimbly conjured up a sack out of newspaper; into it disappeared the "travel provisions" for Ferdinand, the *hombre muy guapo*. The sack vanished elegantly into Ferdinand's jacket pocket, accompanied by a grinning twinkling of his eyes. Pesos deftly changed into the open, withered mushroom hand. Back to the feverish child.

Since this journey, I have pulverized, ground, crushed peppercorns, marjoram, laurel, saffron nuts, garlic in a mortar I bought there; but never chicken claws, ocelot eyes, snake eggs, maguey root, or even dried frog's blood. Yet all these, boiled together into a green, bitter brew, gave Oliver health and immunity for the rest of the trip.

•

The sun rode down behind the black hills. One last flare-up, and the city awakened from its siesta to celebrate the evening. The "evangelists," who wrote letters for those who could not write their own, sat on their heels in the shadow of the church, before them their little tables with an empty chair for the customer. Couples sauntered arm in arm beneath the arcades in the square. The local beauties stepped out from their doors, with blossoms in their hair, blossoms woven into their skirts, their brown skin so golden.

Dueños, the hosts in white shirts, a fatty sheen on their black trousers, cigarettes in the corners of their mouths, stood before their establishments. With their napkins they whacked the afternoon dust from the tables, as a prelude to the night, the gallant seducer. Through the gaps in the leaves above the Plaza Municipal, high in the indigo sky, dragged the tattered smoke tail of an airplane. Maria Felix smiled down from a movie poster: *High Noon*, with Gary Cooper.

We found ourselves in a wild garden that rolled its way down an incline: madrona bushes, strewn with yellow berries. A nervous silver lizard slithered with us from step to step, through lilies, agave, and oleander beds, down toward the illustrious group that had gathered there and now turned to welcome us, full of curiosity.

Bienvenidos, nuestros invitados de Alemania!

Gorgeous mestizos, their faces the color of dark honey, laughed. Men with hair black as enamel demonstrated their virility with the play of their eyebrows, beneath which flashed a brown glance. They wore the national garb of the seducer race: white shirts, black trousers, gleaming patent leather shoes. The women gave a carefree laugh. Beautiful exotic flowers with leisurely movements, they twirled their hair, blossoms nestled within it, played with the little bodice button that pressed their breasts together, stroked their red-nailed hands across their lovers' shoulders as they laughed at their own claim of exclusivity.

From far away, below the horizon, the night beat down on the trees. Mariachi *músicos* serenaded. A typical Mexican feast had been prepared in our honor.

We stood about an indentation in the earth, a kind of grave, covered with banana leaves that kept heat and steam from leaking out. After a certain point, cooks lifted the drunken leaves apart, and the hot air could escape.

And there in the steam lay a whole goat, complete with its fur; it had broiled all day in the glowing hot earth. Quickly and deftly the pelt was stripped off; even the head was skinned, the animal lifted up onto a table. As if in an anatomy class, the steaming cadaver lay before us, as if for the study of its tendons and muscles. The goat eyes stared from glass slits, in dull indifference. The gray tongue protruded from the open mouth.

I surfaced from my shock.

Don't be shy, my pretty, it's a delicacy, someone whispered to me.

We all ate with our hands. Red enameled fingers and male paws clawed at the rib cage. Knives carved. In the belly the sweetbreads lay on aromatic herbs, ready to eat. One took a piece and dipped it in mole, a sour chocolate sauce, black like mole fur. The cook nimbly severed the testicles with a sharp knife. Women shrieked with lust and greed at the symbolism, and on account of the tasty morsel which lay prepared on a plate, cut into thin slices, salted and peppered. The connoisseurs selected the eyes, to suck them dry, the liver, the kidneys. They cut little pieces from the inner thigh.

The goat feast cleared away. It was succeeded by a procession of sweet delicacies: corn cakes glazed with chocolate, *dulce de calabaza*, agave compote, petals dipped in cane sugar, café con leche, and, amidst the delicacies, the senseless skirmish of a conversation, like viscous traffic. Society leaned forward in lazy expectation of something new. Whoever was tired of the music slipped across the meadow, which glowed like crystal in the moist air.

Time rushed across the treetops. The golden moon gaped down upon our intemperance, which Hieronymus Bosch could have painted. Drunken guests lay in hammocks. Someone puked. Couples kissed, intertwined, some voluntarily, others with the faded ribbon of tradition. A few brawlers rolled on the mossy carpet amid the raucous singsong of the musicians. Beneath waxy green leaves others sank into the magical ecstasy of peyote dreams.

Ferdinand had long since given up making sense; nonetheless he directed a story with elegant gestures, as if riding a wave from the unconscious, interrupted by the ritual of licking salt between thumb and forefinger, washing it back with a shot of tequila.

Salud, dinero y tiempo para gastarlo. He laughed, pressed tobacco into the pipe bowl with his finger, lit a match, sucked in the trembling flame, and, without long reflection, resumed tying up the interrupted threads of the story…

Mayahuel, the goddess of drunkenness, came to earth, he called out laughingly, with the fearful spirits of the air, the Tzitzimine, and they ate from the maguey plant. That's how it began. The story leads us to Alva Axthnixochitl, also called Quezalcoatl Ce Acatl Topiltzin…

Ferdinand pronounced every syllable precisely, formed every sound painstakingly with his lips; I knew he was tripping. He had his own voice in his ear, spoke to himself, exhilarated himself with the faces listening to him.

Quezalcoatl is the last king of Tula, son of Tecpancaltzin and his wife Xóchitl. He invented pulque. Pulque from the maguey plant, that has its place in mythology. He looked about him and started to laugh, and laugh, and laugh. He could not get a grip at all, and his listeners laughed with him, a little uncertainly.

From further away, from one of the magnolias, the grating scream of a peacock. Silent geckos rushed up the wall, where, in front of a lantern, a spider spun a net in which pale moths lost their way.

Ferdinand was unstoppable. A glass in one hand, the other arm draped across a guest to prop himself up, he spun his yarn further.

In the time of Tecpancaltzin, among the Toltecs, the noble Papanzin invented the secret. Tlachiqueros prepared the potion. The Aztecs drank pulque during religious ceremonies. He took a deep breath, laughed, his tongue heavy.

Mayahuel, goddess of drunkards... he called out. Tzitzimime, spirit of the breezes Ixtla Octli... my white ecstasy...

He looked out past everyone into the night, patted down the sides of his jacket as if he had forgotten something. Ah, there it is, the pipe, he said, concentrating on his ritual, as if alone.

The night itself was stoned. Laughter hopped about. I drew Ferdinand away with me. Like a spirit, the sweet tone of the pan flute hung above the branches, followed us from stone to stone with its rhythm, on past the whispering oleander and the spider's webs that drew themselves across our faces. Luna moths as big as one's hand swung through shrieking laughter, followed us all the way out to the gate, where the loud company had gathered around waiting cars. Another adventure awaited us.

The corrosive harping of the cicadas was beginning to ebb within the pink wall. Cloud shadows stumbled across the beds of roses, sleepy dogs licked their paws, a figure swept along the wall from the big house to the small.

Oliver slept in our host's house, dreamed beneath the moon that crept through the room, next to his bed a mestiza standing watch.

We clambered into the waiting vehicles, and in a convoy we left the fine precincts of Cuernavaca. Out front the *músicos* led the procession with mariachi songs.

I sat on Ferdinand's lap, squeezed together with other guests. The silent street with its sleeping villas lay behind us.

We raced at breakneck speed along a gravel road, sang loudly and exuberantly, with the musicians out front like spirits on a hair-gray cloud of dust. They crouched at the edge of the open convertible top, and, with every pothole, they flew into the air like weightless straw dolls, in danger of being hurled out at any moment.

In the midst of our ecstatic spectacle, suddenly a gruesome image, which from this point on was an everyday occurrence on this journey. In the middle of the street lay the cadaver of a cow, which the driver had to maneuver around.

A band of crooked-necked carrion vultures lifted off, landing in protest on the branches of a gnarled scotch pine.

Impatient sobering up, and the question of where we were, in fact, driving. Black silhouettes of agave swords stood against a swarm of silverfish clouds. A few straw-covered huts, then on, past artfully heaped tin-can fences, drums of poverty. And there, beneath the sickly light of a streetlamp, we came to a halt in front of a cantina.

Indios lounged wearily about. It smelled of burnt coal, of corn tamales. Behind the roofs of a row of impoverished huts, shone the red flames of tabachin flowers. A few girls leaned sluggishly against a wall, narrowly pressed together: not young, not old, weariness in their eyes. They pressed their breasts between their folded arms. Tired red smiles.

Ah, this was the surprise. We had driven here to gawk. To reward the drinkers drunkenly, with a cheap laugh from a silver-toothed mouth. It was not without its embarrassment, this inconstant magic of coming and going. Ferdinand immediately began photographing. The girls at the doors. Us with the girls at the doors. We laughed, they laughed.

The *muchachas*, younger than they seemed, busy with the primeval experiment of transient happiness, night-soiled faces with guitar figures, slipped out of the background, whispered among themselves:

Guadelupe! Guadelupe, venga, il gringo alemán está. Yo creo que es él?

The view opened up. A saucy young thing with high breasts stood there, one foot pressed against the wall behind her. She lit a cigarette, slowly, took her time. She shook her raven hair and pushed the smoke from her mouth, herself away from the wall, her free hand taking with it the curtain that served as a door, so that for a moment the slice of a mattress painted with dirt could be seen; flimsy, fringed cloths hung in rows across thin metal rods, to protect the sweet indiscriminateness.

Raven Hair Guadeloupe says Aaah, and slowly goes down the few stairs, never letting Ferdinand out of her sight. She comes to a stop, crosses her arms beneath her bosom, and thrusts out her chin.

Aahh, she says again, smilingly sidling up to Ferdinand. She has recognized him. I stare at Ferdinand, at Guadelupe, Guadelupe, Ferdinand.

Ven para aquí, gringo, da me tu... she clicks on the end of an imaginary ballpoint and mimes using it to paint her eyebrows.

She stands quite close to Ferdinand, who has kept hidden in the rectangle of his Hasselblad camera, but is now surfacing, grinning with embarrassment. She puts her arm around his neck, to the applause of the other *putas*, adding to the salty mood of the inexplicable.

She calls Ferdinand *Ixtla octli*, and tickles his ear.

I stand there awkwardly. I steady myself. I fold my arms like Guadalupe. My eyes narrow to slits, trembling, thinking: someone is about to be murdered here.

Ah, yes, says Ferdinand. He gets the message. He laughs broadly and his mouth freezes to a broad grin while he looks for the ballpoint, his broken fingers fumbling tremulously from pocket to pocket on the outside of his suit. He locates it down in his trouser pocket, where she follows him with her mercenary gaze; reaches her the pen, with a handful of notes for them all to share. He makes a sweeping half-moon gesture which the *putas* follow as a dog does a piece of meat dangled before its nose.

Mi esposa, says Ferdinand and points vaguely in my direction, gestures vaguely toward us *gringas*, standing opposite the *putas*.

And my heart stands beside me like a second person.

Yo creo que es él.

Yo creo que es él.

Yo no creo.

The Black Bull

I RUMMAGE AMID THE BONES OF MEMORY, twist and turn the pieces, to place them in the appropriate parts of the puzzle, seek to separate reality and imagination. I can cling firmly only to a few scraps. I remember a feeling of menace, a dark cloud of being handed over to a country full of vicious pranks, hostile to love. A country where Ferdinand, our protector and my betrayer, felt at home, where I could not get out.

There was no intermission between acts.

We were now on our own, Ferdinand, Oliver, and I. Bobsi had departed after the last party.

Take care of yourself, send me a telegram when... I did not let him finish.

I am OK, I said. He held me for a moment and gave me a kiss.

On the trip down from Cuernavaca to the south, the road carried us, within a few hours, from cool mountain weather into the tropics. At the higher altitude the wind beat down on deep woods of dark firs and scotch pines, green meadows dotted with flowers, reminiscent of Bavaria. The clear, cool sliver of daytime moon that dragged along with us, up in the sky, slipped beneath a tangle of clouds and reemerged. Waterfalls fell across mossy cliffs, down steep walls into cold, blue-eyed lakes. Other waters burst from crevices and shot across the roadway. Driving through them we conjured up a glass fan, colored like the kaleidoscope of a rainbow. The road led further down to the temples and burial grounds, which awaited us in the vapor of the jungle air, and, wherever we came to a stop, beneath every hill we drove past, Ferdinand suspected one more hidden treasure of Mexican history.

Ferdinand jerked the steering wheel about. It lifted Oliver and me from our seats. And there, right in front of us, a rabble of carrion vultures squatted on the cadaver of a cow. Screeching, protesting with lazy wings, the birds lifted off, only to land close by on a branch, a fence post.

Only the cows and calves of the poor got run over. They grazed on the narrow strip between the asphalt road and the fencing of the rich landowners. The scrawny beasts were left to their fates, untended.

When we were hungry we would stop at some desolate cantina by the roadside, always next to a clump of huts. There would be poor drunken devils lounging about, their gaze indiscriminate; a few colorful chickens pecking in the dust; dogs, too hungry to bark, pressed up against our legs. I would think of snakes. I could read the thoughts of poverty.

Fifteen minutes or so before one of these stops, we had seen a "dead child" on the shoulder, a bundle of child, smeared with blood, designed to move our compassionate hearts and convince us to stop. However, if we did stop, get out…

But Ferdinand had gone on ahead and already arrived between the Indios at the counter of the cantina. He gestured toward me.

I sprang across a puddle, urine yellow. At its edge a swarm of torpedo wasps drinking, black and poisonous. Crates full of fighting cocks were stacked up against the wall of a hut. A handful of women squatted on the floor a little further off. The Indios grinned, shy and embarrassed on account of us, we who did not belong here. They freed up the view of the foods that lay on palm leaves beneath wire nets: *tortillas con queso asadero* and *sopa de chorizo*, blood sausage, also *sopa di pollo*. The food, laid out in the moist heat, had probably been waiting to be eaten for days.

Ferdinand chatted with the Indios, whom he overtowered by two heads, drank a glass of mescal with them, a glass of pulque, toasted amid their grins, thus freeing them from the overwhelming difference. I too had to take a swig, for the sake of disinfection. Oliver had already gulped down his whipped-up brew from the Cuernavaca market that morning for the same reason.

I went over to the women and let them know, with hand gestures, that Oliver was five years old, and they smiled contentedly, for he was already as large as their ten-year-olds. Beneath a banana tree I allowed myself to be embraced by the magic of the strange innocence in their gentle faces, and sat down with them, while Oliver joined a mechanic who lay beneath an almost unrecognizable pickup truck.

I bought a grubby serape, a cape, finely woven, in green, white, and black, which I own to this day. The weaving was from this region and astonishingly elegant. I also bought a little printed kerchief that looked as if it were from home. I could not explain it to them, but I had to laugh, and they laughed along with me. And their laughter drove away my thoughts. For a brief while I forgot the barbaric instruments of their hopelessness. Amid the carefree skirmishing over by the liquor bottles, where the men were standing, the menace I had sensed was distorted into something ridiculous, that bloody bundle we had seen on the road into a figment of tourists' imaginations. Must have been an error…although, that little foot…

I was sick at my stomach.

Ferdinand was smoking peyote in a tortoise-shell pipe, busy falling back into his old rhythm. He was in the best of moods, while darkness reached out for him again. Only I seemed to see it.

I was sick at my stomach.

He called me a spoilsport, had no wish to look into any shitty mirror; I was to quit being hysterical and enjoy soaking up Mexico:

You just need a good night's sleep…

Quién sabe was the Indios' grinning response to the question of how far it was to the next city, the next hotel. One of them peered far out over the tips of the trees, skeptically lowered the corners of his mouth.

On foot it takes a whole day to get there, he said.

One of the others, wanting to be courteous, answered our question with a broad grin, said it was only an hour.

Yet another, presumably a poet, had once gone there on the bus. As the sun disappeared at the end of the sky with the energy of a gentle lightning bolt, he had climbed off there in the city.

Was it that day, or one of the following, when we arrived in the city? Was it the city of San Andrés Tuxtla, perhaps, or Villahermosa? All I can still remember is the majestic rain that pounded down between the parked cars, and the few meters to the entrance of our hotel, which we ran in through, soaked naked.

The sole window was in the room that served as bathroom, the toilet a hole in the floor with a water pitcher and a decrepit broom next to it. The sole bed stood musty and dark beneath a crucified Savior, pierced with arrows. In the corners, plundered tangles of dust and hair. Up above, on the ceiling, a lonely bulb with a cord I pulled at night to have some light, an action that sent me shrieking back into bed. Hundreds of cockroaches, as big as mice, scurried through the room, racing into the toilet hole. Nothing could bring me to use the horrid pit for my purposes. Ferdinand had to accompany me down to the street, where a few bushes embraced one another for my protection.

We traveled on. Dusty green agave plantings by the roadway. Banana shrubs, buckling under their load. Peacocks, whose regal elegance underlined the poverty of a hut housing a large family. Fences made of tin cans. Behind one of them yelped a chihuahua, pegged up like a piglet on a very short leash, with only a tiny radius of movement, to fatten it up.

I saw an ocelot hovering in the interwoven green, monsoon-drenched, saw the spotted paw, the amber gaze. Or was it just the play of light and shadow? *Quién sabe?*

A burro, laden with a sack and a drunkard riding on top of it, led by his pregnant wife, she with a child on her back. And on this trip I really did see the *Árbol del Tule*, said to be the widest tree in the world.

And what do you think lay next to this giant? A bundle of onions and four potatoes, for sale on a palm leaf.

At one point there was a woman standing in a field, alone, harvesting ears of corn. We stopped to photograph her. She turned toward us, with a despairing expression on her face, and her hand gestures told us not to come any closer. With a groan she suddenly bent forward, her legs planted widely on the ground, and pulled the hem of her skirt up between her thighs. Once again a loud groan that carried all the way over to us, followed by a pained moan. Another moan, more suppressed, as if she were holding her hand in front of her mouth, and, immediately after it, the sweet redeemed cry of a newborn child. She held the bundle out before her on her arm, bent down, and bit through the umbilical cord. With tired steps, she withdrew from us across the parched corn, slowly toward the forest. Her dress red with the blood of the birth, she disappeared behind the curtain of trees, taking with her the story we could scarcely believe.

•

San Cristóbal de las Casas, a colonial city. White-chalked steps lead up to a white church. Rural and broad, of a moving primitiveness. Not like the baroque churches in Bavaria, pompously decorated for the glory of God. Here the churches were the place to meet, and not only for the Christian God; other divinities too had their places of worship there. *Quién sabe*, who really knows, which god is in charge of the crops, of the weather, of health?

In San Cristóbal we were guests of Gertrude Blom, whom Ferdinand knew from earlier travels. We stayed in her wonderful dark house, a former convent, rectangular, with a quiet interior courtyard where even the orange blossoms seemed to whisper. In the evening an Indio, clad in white, silent, with soft movements—they seemed as much a part of him as his brown skin —brought into the room a basin of coal, whose orange-red heart glowed through the cold night. He bowed with a smile, gestured, indefinite as a cloud.

With the morning the scent of vanilla and jasmine climbed through the iron bars of the window, datura bushes softly shook their giant bells in the fresh air of the higher altitudes. In the center, in the tiled inner courtyard, stood a huge head of clay, across whose sleeping smile water ran and ran, in the incessant rhyme of the day and the night.

Gertrude Blom was a strict lady from Switzerland whom fate had tossed up on these shores. Her husband, Franz Blom, studied the Lacandon Indians, who still lived untouched and cordoned off from the rest of Mexico. In the course of his research he lifted a boy out of his life in the jungle, took him in, sent him to school: both to learn reading and Spanish and as an experiment, to determine how far he was able and willing to learn. They called him Nablom.

At the Casa Blom the guests had to appear punctually at the communal table. After the exuberant greeting, meant mainly for Ferdinand and Oliver, Gertrude finally held out her hand to me, her glance inspecting, brief, and imperious. I felt right away that she tolerated me as one does a well-trained dog, worthy of no further notice, although her gaze magically wandered over to me again and again. I lit a cigarette and puffed out a smokescreen between Gertude and me.

Gertrude reigned at the head of the table. The scent of corn was in the air. On hand-painted ceramic plates lay red beans with green peppers, red and golden tomatoes, rice and fish, papaya, quesadillas with *queso Oaxoca*. On the furnishings beneath the domed ceiling, a celebration of the garden outside: vases of sunflowers, dahlias and red poppy, blossoms like crumpled paper, with a black stamp of marzipan.

Gertrude cut such a stately figure that my mind's eye places two Dobermans at her side, ears perked, in the unison of dignitaries, attentively following the political power games at the table above.

Blue hydrangeas with fiery red gladiolas sat grandly in the centerpiece, so that I could hide behind them and laugh with the guests next to me about the bus ride from San Cristóbal de las Casas to Teopisca.

During that journey we'd rattled along on bumpy gravel roads, praying the engine would make it, the oncoming trucks so near we could touch them with our outstretched hands. Squatting and standing with us in the bus were mestizos and Indios, their Aztec ancestors stamped into their profiles, some of them drunk. Live turkeys and whole gaggles of chickens had been hung up by their feet, tranquilized, their heads dangling. Women with stoic gazes, colorful ribbons woven through their hair, held their babies in cloths wound about their torsos. With horror I saw lice out for a walk on their thick braids. I did not move, held Oliver firmly in my lap, and could only hope not to make the acquaintance of the classless vermin on this trip.

Once again the road was lined with straw-covered huts, nailed together with tin, their doors made from scraps, and always, among the colorful hens, a little chihuahua tethered to a peg to fatten up. And then finally the vista opened onto the reward for the beat-up journey: a white baroque church, and on the wide plaza in front, a billowing crowd, a fiesta.

We entered the church. Fir needles lay on the floor, a thick soft carpet. Families with children danced and trampled around on them. Shrouded in the streaming aroma, almost numbed, we staggered back out onto the plaza. Mariachis were playing; noise spurted like a cloudburst from the tin instruments and the deafening uproar of the crowd overcame us.

The men—you could see how macho they felt—wore short, white trousers cut off at the knees, white shirts with ponchos slung over their shoulders, tied together in the middle; on their heads, straw hats at a rakish angle. Women in wildly colored woven dresses stirred beans and chile in steaming clay pots. Tortillas and corncobs roasted on open fires. All reminiscent of a Rivera tableau, against the backdrop of a gnarled green landscape.

And again, here too, the oppressive, threatening feeling of danger, of the nullity of life—a perpetual state of intoxication. From every direction firecrackers and rockets, *fuegos artificiales*, swept through the air right past the heads of the crowd, of grownups and children, ceaselessly, wildly, drunkenly set off by dilettantes using their hands as torches, never giving the danger a second's thought. There was little that one would put past the black tufts of raven hair, the low foreheads, and the constant grin: the mark of the fatalist.

And then once again, right next to all the wildness, this piece of astonishment, of surprise: a tableau of silent beauty. Persimmons next to a few apples on a carpet woven red, green, and yellow. I bought the still life with the carpet thrown in. A broad, childlike smile thanked me for it.

As soon as the mayor, *Principales de la Ciudad*, discovered us, he came running, waving his hands, extremely considerate. With his twirled mustache he looked like Emilio Zapata. Conscious of his important position, he wanted to show us around.

Vengan, les quiero mostrar algo! He waved.

He proudly pointed out the reservoir, a cinderblock disgrace next to some palms; and in the same gesture, the high mountain train in the distance, where I could make out a waterfall between the undergrowth and the sky.

But now he wanted to take us to the local sensation. It was ten years ago that a group of gringos had come from the USA and built toilets for the town. He nodded thoughtfully as he led us along a road full of potholes. He seemed not altogether satisfied with the sensation.

We left the last row of huts behind us and stood hard at the edge of the highland jungle. There, beneath an extended roof that only weakly resisted a robust climbing shrub, stood a long wooden bench with a backrest and four holes of varying size cut into the seat, one after another.

He pointed down into the deep black blackness filled with water. He was a man of progressive convictions; it would be lovely if the toilets were used; but as things stood... he shrugged his shoulders in resigned helplessness.

It is uncommonly tragic, he said, pointing, a despairing, hopeless smile on his face. No one wishes to use the toilets, as we lost one of our children down there.

No fence, no door separated the place of privacy from the public eye. From the forest, the buzzing of bees, the shrieking of birds; from the town, the boom of exploding poverty, together with the laughter of aristocrats. Those of us at the table in Gertrude Blom's house also had to laugh at the tragicomic typicality of this Mexican event.

The hospitable meal leaned toward its end with sweets: chocoflan, papaya, little pink bananas. And yet the superb evening was not willing to die. Ferdinand lifted himself and his glass: to celebrate Gertrude, the Lacandon Indians, the festive, colorful table. His words reeled; he laughed, and as if dizzy he staggered backward until he felt the wall. With a sigh he opened the heavy book he held in his hand, his place already marked with his forefinger. The sacred book of the Quiché. He wanted to read us something more:

...There was as yet nothing that was together, nothing that made a sound, also nothing that moved, lived, or made a noise in the sky.

There was nothing, only the silent water, the gentle sea, lonely and calm. Nothing was there.

There was only immobility, the silence of darkness and night. Only the creator and shaper Tepeu, Gucumatz; Mother and Father were in the water.

Surrounded by light, wrapped in green-and-blue feathers he was, and that is why he is called Gucumatz.

They were great wise men and great thinkers.

And there was the sky and also the "heart of the sky," which is the name of the gods, which they gave themselves.

Then came the Word. Tepeu and Gucumatz came together in the darkness, in the night; and Tepeu and Gucumatz spoke with one another. They spoke reflectively and with consideration. They found their way to one another. They married their words and thoughts.

And as they thought thus, it became clear to them:

When dawn breaks, mankind must appear...

I did not want to look over at him, to see how he stood there at the wall, reaching for a grip. I wanted only to let into myself the words that pleased me so much.

For a moment it was quiet in the room. Candles threw serpent shadows across the table. The groaning of a chair, pushed back, broke the silence; then applause fell across the remains of the meal. Everyone loved Ferdinand. For once again he had achieved his cherished goal, offering them their own history as theatre. This was an evening where everyone was drunk. A festive mood emanated from the good food, from the lively conversation. From up above, the hand of the fan swatted at us with its shadow. But once the presentation was over, Ferdinand seemed lonely, lost.

Later, in bed, my ears perked up. Across the wall clambered the voices of the night, thickly woven like a carpet. Toads inflated themselves beneath leaves, peacocks took fright, guineas clucked and bickered. Birds chattered. An owl signaled: Uuuhuuu. It had clawed up a rat.

From way down below, music, sweet and tinny. It smelled like tamales. Sister Moon, Brother Darkness, Narcissus in my narrow bed, roped together with me, god of seduction, pain and pleasure.

I could not hold it back. Out of rage and love I wept for Ferdinand. Damn you, Mayahuel, you fucking slut.

I freed myself from his sex, peeled myself from his arm. Ferdinand rolled like a lead weight into the resulting empty space. I hated our drunken act of lust. And at the same time I had boundless longing for intimacy, which pressed itself against me in the sole available form of his firm alcoholized member.

I left the bed and stepped to the window. Bats flew across to the black park. In the east the sky was already pink. My hand lay forgotten on the edge of a bookshelf. As I accidentally bumped into a book, dust flew up. Generations of silverfish had gnawed through the convent library.

•

The smallest of airports, sawed into the thick wall of the jungle. Ferdinand, Oliver, and I waited around, like the silence itself. A few hornet Cessnas dozed in the sun. Indios squatted next to a little house where the air-traffic controls were gathering dust. The electric wire ran through the window, climbed high onto a pole, and lost itself in the tangled foliage.

Our pilot was a good-for-nothing, his unsteady gaze gave him away. One could smell it, too. He had shoved his pilot's cap far out from his forehead; it stuck way back on his bushy black hair. A warning. A flask was wedged into his rear trouser pocket. He grinned across to us with long rabbit teeth, colored rusty brown by tobacco and betel nuts.

A thrilled Ferdinand danced around this fellow. He had negotiated with Gonzales until he could afford the flight to Yucatán, the "land of the pheasant and the stag."

Return ticket, Ferdinand grinned, stowed away his camera equipment, then Oliver and me, behind his seat, next to the pilot.

Now for the scraping out of the pipe: tap it on the step of the Cessna, pull the tobacco pouch from his pocket, stuff the pipe anew, press it into the bowl of the pipe, light it.

In the corner of Gonzales's mouth hung a cigarette, and, with a canister of gasoline in his hand, he went about filling the plane's tank, puffing, one eye squinting.

Tú estás borracho? I shrieked, seized Oliver, and jumped out of the aircraft.

You idiot! Take that cigarette out of your mouth!

Which he then did with a grin, flicking the burning butt across to the tank full of gasoline.

Oliver and I once again sat in the aircraft. Outside, Gonzales held Ferdinand firmly by the arm, pulled his flask of Chichaschnapps from his rear pocket—he couldn't sit down otherwise, he gestured laughingly— and reached Ferdinand a drink. Both took a big slug.

Caramba! They toasted one another, and once again they all looked alike: Ferdinand, Gonzales, the captain on the ship, their fatalistic grin.

He flies better that way, Ferdinand leaned back to laugh to me. I know it from myself.

And already the plane was rumbling off across the muddy runway. Oliver laughed and could barely contain his joy. Scarcely had we lifted off above the tips of the trees when I had to hand Ferdinand his camera equipment.

Beneath us in the woven carpet of the *chicozapotes* nestled the ruined city of Palenque. Ferdinand took photos. The shadow of our Cessna stroked across the Temple of Inscriptions, the little Temple of the Sun, the Palace, the Tower, and right after that the red snake of the Usumacinta River cut through the end-less green tangle.

I prayed to Itab, goddess of suicides; to the two-headed dragon Itzamna, with the serpent body, whose skull devours the day in the west; to the war god Ekchuah, who spurts blood across a cliff—blood—spurt—oh God, it was my veins the blood was spurting through! We were racing toward a rock wall that climbed from the flatlands with a sudden start!

In the nick of time, our pilot jerked the aircraft up. In his slow-motion haze of drunkenness he had barely seen the emergency coming.

Ferdinand took photos, turned back to us with a grin, as if nothing had happened. And Gonzales, to get himself back into the groove, knocked back a big swig from his flask. Ferdinand shouted something over to him, and the air-craft obeyed. We whizzed downward, flying inches above the treetops. Oliver was jubilant; I was ready to vomit.

Memory flows in scraps, like clouds in an atmospheric storm. We survived the insane flight, though Ferdinand had to swear an oath that this would be the last we undertook. For our journey across the Yucatán peninsula we transferred to a Jeep.

This time our chauffeur was Miguel, yet another in the same genre of drunkard. His silver tooth glittered dangerously when he laughed.

I saw everything; my hearing, too, had grown sharper, pointed like the pen of a chronicler. I was the forensic detective who sinks his claws deep into his case, follows everything with the greatest exactitude. This was not my journey, not my country. It was Ferdinand's heart's blood. Here, even his drinking became a celebration. *Borracho*! What a masculine word. The starter that got the machine rolling…He loved the Spanish language, loved the complicated words and names of the past. They were his mental calisthenics. Even when he was already staggering he could recite the alphabet of his obsession like a prayer.

It seemed only I saw the child in the grubby red dress, beneath a clove tree, who offered us a puppy for sale, a chihuahua ready for slaughter. Only I noticed the blue frock, the naked foot, the bloody bundle at the curb. The woman on the bus—was she not Guadelupe, the whore? Take a look, have I got lice in my hair now? There—our pilot Gonzales lies crucified in the street…

These horrors I saw, and beauties too: saw the thousand shadows of the elephant trunks of the rain god Chac that flowed along the wall of Codz Pop; saw how pink evening clouds twisted in the sky, an airy image of the temple façade; saw in this moment a woman clad in white Yucatán garb approaching us from the tangle of climbing shrubs, without paying us the slightest notice. She came to a stop at the wall, pulled on a rope, and filled her vessel with water. The miracle of a fountain that had existed there for centuries. It would have been ungracious to address her, and she would not have answered. Thus her appearance was that of a dove, for a few silken minutes reconciling the gods with everything destructive, until the sun set and we awakened from the beholding.

There. in the temple of the soothsayer, sits the dwarf of Uxmal, whom the people anointed their king. In a watering hole on the bank of an underground river, an old woman squats by a serpent. She sells water in exchange for newborn children, whom she feeds to the serpent. This old woman is the dwarf's mother…

I found the photos from this journey in a book Ferdinand dedicated to Franz Blom. Not to Gertrude! I love this book. It is non-linear, and yet it narrates the whole saga of *The Maya and Their Art*. And precisely because of its unusual structure, it contains equal amounts of speculation and truth.

·

We came to a village where they were making the preparations for a *feria*. A crowd had gathered where an arena had been built up in front of the ruins of a pyramid. The main attraction was a bullfight that was to take place there. The sickly-sweet old odor of cooked corn hovered heavily in the air. We hung around waiting with the crowd, whom we towered above by almost two heads. Intoxicated and full of excitement, they paid us scant notice.

Finally the time had come, and the matador strode into the ring, accompanied by shouting and loud music. The bullfight itself was a rural, clownish circus performance. The skinny little bull was scarcely in a position to fight. Inadequacy, ambiguity hovered above the tumult. And I was afraid. I held Oliver's hand firmly, for I experienced the unpredictable chaos as the overture to an impending tragedy. My tallness and white skin protected me, but they could just as well prove my downfall. One never knew.

Ferdinand had written in one of his books: *The forces of nature are wasteful, or they withhold from mankind what is most necessary. The gods change their sex, are now masculine, now feminine, and then both at the same time. They slip into the skin of an animal or take on human form. They speak to humans as the dead or as the living, and on top of it they lead armies of powerful, beneficent, or sometimes wicked sub-gods.*

Yes, I felt this duality, the incalculable. Human beings are delivered up to themselves, defenseless, pressed into a corner, like the skinny little bull all the shrieking was about.

A murderous rage hovered over the madding crowd, betrayed into its own hands. At the same time one sensed deep, helpless sorrow.

And Ferdinand was like a prince of the Indios, his blood bound up with their blood. He could have been naked, held a serpent in his hand, a jaguar at his side, and it would not have put them off. On the contrary, they would have celebrated him. Also, like them he was drunk on pulque, gazing with the same glassy stare upon the horrid beauty of the ceremony.

He photographed, documented, like a man possessed. It was hot. One could reach out and grasp the thick dust all around. Slate-gray clouds hung low in a sky full of rain. On this day, too, one could measure the instant of discharge with the exactitude of a Swiss watch. Camera equipment in hand, we raced to the car; scarcely had we arrived when the rain cut loose and poured down.

Rain pounded on the tin roof of our Jeep. Rust-red dust danced everywhere. As I looked back, a few Indios stood there like spirits in short white trousers, with *serapes* tossed across their shoulders, and also there quite tenderly, now recognizable only as a pencil sketch, the little black bull.

I kept this grotesque in my memory—the skinny bull, the arena in the middle of the nowhere jungle, the shabbily dressed matador, the thrilled blasting of fireworks that accompanied every party and had often devoured the last money a paterfamilias possessed. Yes, I saw everything, and I felt the monstrosity, the prophecies, the darkness that Ferdinand shared with them. Colonial Mexico lived on. Silence was only apparent, and the noise of their festivities could just as well have been martial thundering.

The Castillo

I am the spirit that always negates;
For everything that comes into existence
Is worthy of going to ruin...

—Goethe, *Faust: Part 1*

MERIDA OR CAMPECHE, I was not certain which town we had arrived in. I felt terribly tired, heavy as stone. My heart was heavy. The longing for little Daniel, the daily worry about worry, sucked and tore away at me. I had now seen enough to understand, was much further away from innocence, from good faith, than ever before. I no longer believed myself strong and immune to my fate. I was mistrustful, like an abused dog, cautious, like a wounded child, shaken awake by impatience and by the sensitivity of mimosas. And I kept thinking: every act of forgiveness is the hope of a promise.

Yes, yes, I thought that way. Ferdinand promised nothing.

I was fighting for a sunken realm, the realm of my hopes, while Ferdinand was living, indeed ruling in the sunken realm of the Mayans, the Aztecs, the Incas, together with the accursed Mayahuel.

Ferdinand promised nothing.

We took a rest stop in this small, wonderfully beautiful colonial city. An ancient Spanish settlement from the time of Cortés's conquest offered us a pretty hotel. Bougainvilleas, white and magenta, dreamed their way up the walls. Palms surrounded the plaza. Under a pearly sky Oliver and I sat in the carpet

of shadow beneath hibiscus blossoms and spooned up leche-asada-flan. All around us grand white colonial edifices, remains of a fortification. The city was surrounded by ruins and as-yet-unexcavated hills from the time of the Maya and the Toltecs. There was one place called Tacoh Hopalchén, jaguar scat. The name lets me remember it to this day. And there, too, quite nearby, lay the palace Codz Pop, the house of masks and of the rain god, the place that bestowed upon us the apparition of the woman in white who dipped down into the water.

But where was Ferdinand? He dropped us off somewhere and disappeared, just as he did at home, down the stairs, into the dark corridor below, he vanished through the ribs of the foreign surroundings, the soft, brown faces, slipped away, between walls, through mysterious colonial doors, beneath barricades of bougainvillea. The camera was his alibi.

There exists no photograph capturing the three of us together. Like a fugitive he plundered the feelings of those who loved him. Then, unexpectedly, Ferdinand surfaced again, his pockets bulging with *idoles*. As if he had made a side trip to visit Mephisto, he also stuffed in the magic potions and betel nuts that dissolved his scruples.

Mescal, mescal, the witches whispered.

We made our way through the city like tourists. In the baroque churches stood martyred saints, reminiscent of Otto Dix drawings, whose bloody ardor proclaimed them relatives of the gods from the time before the conquest. There was a saint and a name-day for every conceivable suffering in the human tragedy. Maria's heart bled in her open blouse; Lazarus dragged his tormented body along on crutches, gray and more dead than alive. Christ streamed red with blood, pierced with thorns and arrows; from the wounds in the middle of his outstretched hands shot sunbeams like a present for his pains. Sinners impaled on tree stumps; snakes that hid in skulls. A picture-book of horror, gaily colored, full of macabre lyricism.

Rows of *idoles* stood in the bakeries, sacrifices for the saints' name-days: skulls made of sugar icing, skeletons in every color. In the streets, in niches within houses, stood small, intimate altars called *descansos*, adorned with plastic flowers and graced with every possible comestible. The sugary dead melted in the heat; whole battalions of ants dragged off the remains, like the sins of the penitents.

We had a pink church, the most joyous Mexican-operetta interpretation of the Christian faith, packed up in a crate to send home.

Oh, and scarcely had we exited the church portal onto the sunny plaza when we were offered the old gods, who presided over the imaginary forces of nature and are responsible for them to this day.

The God of the Christians cannot keep an eye on everything, said Jesus, the Indio who crisscrossed the archeologically overabundant landscape with Ferdinand. One divine being alone cannot be everywhere, cannot have made everything, not be responsible for everything. Jesus invoked the presiding gods before every hill and every river crossing, bowed low, piled up several stones, and spent a few minutes in prayer.

¿Hola gringo, quieres idoles?

Children held little clay figures in their hands, rummaged in their pockets for shards, and quickly the news had made the rounds that Ferdinand was a *loco* who bought *idoles*. And sometimes a particularly fine ceramic work stumbled in among the little heads and shards. Ferdinand tapped, cocked an ear, scratched with his thumbnail, and asked the Indio, who put on a friendly poker face:

Where did you get it?

From my father.

Ferdinand gave him a skeptical look.

Oh, that is much older than life itself, said the boy with a sly grin.

How long did it take your father to make it?

Siete días, señor.

Ferdinand had written in his book: *they are masterful forgers, their hands are guided by the deeply-rooted belief in the gods of nature and by the fear of them. As one enters the temple, between the reliefs, the remains of walls, the steps, the pillars, it begins to come alive. These are the witnesses of colonial history, thrown together by a monumental error of circumstance. They are the ever-present visions, anonymous and enigmatic, burned into the memory.*

Under the moody light of an insane storm—flashes of lightning that cut through the clouds like shots—I read a poem to the "masters of the forest." It came from the era of Christianization and is still recited in prayer before the hunt:

> *Today I have come before*
> *Your face, Pokohil,*
> *on your day, 4 Ish,*
> *we have come....*
> *We bring one-and-a-half-hundred slices*
> *Of our Copal with us.*
> *Do us a friendliness,*
> *Give us one of your stags,*
> *Bestow upon us one of your animals....*
> *For this I bring our floral sacrifice...*
> *You who are mother and father to us.*

With every temple we entered, something jumped us, as if it were a living creature. Not that the brain really registered it; no, it crept into your soul, took possession; it was just this history that had been "thrown together by a monumental error of circumstance."

Sublime priests with murderous gazes presented on platters the sacrificial gifts, with quetzal birds dancing round about. Ocarina's sweet tones breathed accompaniment. The gifts existed in many forms: a sitting woman, a bird, a jaguar. Vessels decorated with ape heads stood on woven mats, filled with wondrous fruits that thrived only here. A mother with children fixed tortillas. At the pillars, warriors crouched together; or they lay in the grass, their arms outstretched as if on a crucifix. Hundreds of stone skulls decorated a wall; Chac the rain god appeared, a vessel of yellow clay; red stars danced round about a child god who lifted his arms high; grinning apes surrounded a sacrificial font; chasubles in human form pushed smoke from mouth and eyes; the clay doll lay on the step, limbs bound with an ancient plant fiber. In niches, turned away from the light of day, hundreds of bats hung pressed together, blind as old leaves.

•

I awoke suddenly, startled by a new noise that had joined the familiar hum of the night. Rain pounded down on tin, like a clenched fist. I tapped about with my eyes in the hotel room. Blind light from outside. I probed for Ferdinand's body. The bed beside me was empty.

Fucking hell, always the same thing.

The fan hung above the bed like a black nightmare. Ah, no electricity. As the three of us fell asleep it was still spinning, casting its shadow on the ceiling with a sickly beat of its wings.

I could sense the heap of ocelot furs on the table. In the moist air the furs stank of decomposition. They had come into our possession together with a number of *idoles*, in exchange for a handful of dollar notes.

After a long search, I found a candle and, after using up a whole box of soggy matches, finally got it lit. On the table, and everywhere else, lay hands, hearts, legs, also metal torsos with the lacing of heart, lungs, liver, and stomach— the artifacts that Ferdinand bought everywhere we went. They were votives, like the ones hanging in the churches, stamped from silvery tin, fitted out with thank-you letters for the healing of an illness or an injured limb, or the safe return of a lost husband—or the loss of a returned one…

Oliver slept deeply, enwrapped in dreams, did not hear the rain nor the shouting down on the plaza, which brought me to the window. Palms bent in the silver-light skirts of the lanterns. Opposite, beneath the arcades, a few silhouettes lurked against the glum lighting of a bar. Rain, rain, and a few piano keys.

And here, because I kept having to think of Goethe's Mephisto, I also kept thinking of Goethe's Gretchen. Squinting, I tried to penetrate the shrine of the rain, peer across to the temple of drunkards, sought the familiar profile, with the pipe in its mouth. I wished to peel away that form and eliminate everything else, to pose myself Gretchen's question, whose answer I long since knew, but had to have confirmed so many times:

> *That overwhelms me so greatly,*
> *That, wherever he cares so much as to step over to us,*
> *I even think my love for you is gone…*

I stood in this dark room, in which only an angry candle flickered, and peeled my ears and squinted my eyes by the window, waiting, thinking. I gathered, piled up, counted, weighed, for I could not grasp it. Does happiness—do I, do the children—carry so little weight? And does the mistress Mayahuel, goddess of drunkards, who opens her mouth as if it's her sex, carry that much more?

Once again I heard an alienating noise, this time at my back, away from the torrent of rain that I had already caught in my ear, had already known forever. No, now, at the door, a clattering fall, something scraped along the wooden pane, then a moaning.

I could open the door only a crack. Something was leaning against it from

the outside: the ceremony of my reality. Ferdinand was lying on the stone floor, his head pressed against the wooden doorframe. His mouth hung open, his breath deep and heavy; next to the limp hand, between his outstretched legs, lay the key. I squeezed through the crack, could tug his heavy body away from the door only with great effort. Ferdinand murmured and reflexively defended himself.

Oh, qué lástima. El señor está muy borracho, laughed a voice next to me.

It was our host, a mestizo in white trousers, naked torso, disheveled night hair. I could imagine what he was thinking, woken up by the tumult; and also, that for him it was an everyday, or rather an every-night, event—he did not seem in the least embarrassed. Owing to his semi-nudity and the intimate perspective, there stood something impudent in his face, a sort of disgusting confidentiality toward me. The night, and the fact that we were both wearing very few clothes, struck him as a challenge. He laughed broadly, heaved Ferdinand up under the armpits, and hauled him into our room.

I laid a pillow on the floor and covered Ferdinand.

Buenas noches, I said loud and clear, without looking at our host, and pushed the door shut behind him.

Ferdinand groaned in his sleep. From the bubbling depth of a volcano, he carried on an angry conversation with his birth demons.

I lay in the bed, weeping and enraged. I was afraid of my powerlessness and my disappointment. I had to bring a silver votive heart in a *descanso*, a sugar skeleton, too, and write on a scrap of paper:

Here died love

Old thoughts revealed themselves. Scraps of conversation—the worried glance at one's back hits like a spoken warning—Ferdinand, the daily egg is not enough—my father laughs—the hearty, almost-convinced: You two have my blessing—Ferdinand grins, next to him the suitcase—Just sell the gold bars if the money runs out—the scream of Daniel, just born, for me alone. Also: Ferdinand kneels before me, a gentle gesture that makes me happy, makes me gather in the instant of remorse; but that remorse evaporates immediately, like rain on hot asphalt, because I know he is looking at the wall of books.

Ah, there it is, I've looked for it for ages. The view through the window, across the tin roof down onto the street corner, reveals nothing. The brotherliness with the Captain, conjured forth from a Georg Grosz drawing—information, as indestructible as plastic—the steaming of the ship, and night breaking across it—

Verbal tatters danced about each picture, until it grew so dense that I suppose I must have fallen asleep.

•

During this liquid time, on this journey, contact with origins, people, and perspectives went missing. The intoxicating light in which we modulated our lives was joined by uncertainty, old, long-repressed fear, rage. Hard, ugly cartilages formed, and I no longer buried them in silence.

It was perhaps the lack of shame that really revealed the shredding of Ferdinand's personality. I stood there, helpless in the face of his addiction to any and every kind of altered state. It was like war. Awoken from his alcoholic faint, he would momentarily be back in contact with the dignity of his wide-ranging education. I was fighting with weapons that he shoved aside with the adroitness of a karate warrior, until they slid off into the ridiculous.

> *I am the spirit that always negates…*
> *So that was the core of the poodle,*
> *A wandering scholastic? The case makes me laugh.*
> *That is how everything you call sin, destruction—in a word, evil—*
> *Is my proper element.*

He had never apologized for the whore Guadelupe. Given his absolute ignorance as to feelings of shame, particularly in this world of machos, I took his shame upon myself. I was ashamed for him, twisted his behavior into my source of pride, was simply too big-hearted for my defeat. Guadelupe was part of the ceremonial form he claimed for himself. In moments of self-knowledge he was almost ripe for repentance, yet ranked this as weakness and reached once again for his elixirs, tequila and peyote, falling back into the certainty of his arrogance.

After our botched relaxation in the lovely city, we got moving again with our guide Miguel, though I was so fed up that Ferdinand practically had to drag me along. How I felt did not concern him. He was obsessed with showing me Chichen Itza. We had to share it with him; otherwise the trip would lack a climax. Ferdinand overcame my scruples with charm and boundless passion: My God, you will never be here again…

At this moment his excitement made him the more reasonable of the two of us. And there were no witnesses.

•

We were like Chicleros hunting for chicozapote trees. We were in search of the rain god Chac; the serpent prince Ah Kin Mai; Ah Puch, the god of death; we were searching for the Castillo of Quetzalcoatl-Kukulcan.

Are there really toads here as big as chickens? And what is the deal with these spiders as big as eggs, and with the poisonous snakes? I looked with questioning horror into the densely packed green jungle wall, and pushed the cuffs of my riding trousers into my high leather boots.

Quién sabe? answered Miguel, the idiot, and laughed, unconcerned and moronic.

Ferdinand was already walking on ahead. Oliver and an entire horde of little Indian boys carried his cameras, his stand, his rolled-up paper, and his paints. These were the tools he wanted to use for rubbings.

Before us lay the Plateau of Venus; the Plateau of the Skulls surrounded the Temple of Warriors with its thousand pillars, the Castillo, the marketplace, the observatory. The ruined city hummed in total isolation. Looking as if one could walk upon it, an impenetrable carpet of tree and underbrush wove its way about the temple grounds out to the horizon. As far as the eye could see, no hills, nothing, only the wickerwork of the jungle, above it the woven fabric of the clouds. On the horizon, a ring of dust, and, as messengers, the black crosses of the swallows swooping about.

A still breeze lifted and turned over the nearby leaves, rust-red and gray. Mimosa plumage preened itself lemon yellow next to a ruin. Beyond was blackness and silence. Only the repetitive cry of a beast, perhaps a bird, like a cry for help. Cloud cover, spooled up by the hours, drew across the great pyramid.

Ferdinand had already been here in Chichen Itza, in this violent city of the Toltecs, several times. Giving precise directions in Spanish, he led the children with their burdens toward a stone wall bearing a relief of a ballplayer. Behind his hat, the smoke escaped his pipe in short, strained puffs. The children held a big piece of paper up to the wall, and Ferdinand pressed against it with a sponge dipped in paint. When he was done the little troupe moved on to the next relief. As soon as the paper was dry, one could roll it up. These were Ferdinand's finds, which could easily be carried along.

I took off on my own toward Tzompantli, the Platform of the Skulls, and on past the jostling row of gargoyles, past the little Temple of Venus, left the steps adorned with serpent gods, their maws gaping wide. I entered the big ball field with towering walls. On a stone relief, warriors danced around the plaza. Skulls pressed in upon one another. The devouring jaws of the Plumed Serpent grinned down upon me. Ballplayers wore jaguar masks, struggling with their own sacrificial death. I felt a bit player in this gigantic arena, which supposedly could hurl my echo back at me eightfold. And yet I did not wish to call out, not even whisper, for even whispering would have carried the frightful echo further.

I stood there, quite still. I felt myself tattooed by the blood-drenched history: *that was to appease the gods, put them in a merciful mood, the same gods that one day were to fail and abandon Indian culture to its downfall.* I felt the density of mystery round about me, and went slowly toward the Castillo. Ninety-one stairs, in each of the four directions of the compass: 364 altogether, and one extra stair, to complete the days of the solar year. I climbed every step and counted.

High above me on the plateau stood the shrine. Witches made of gray cloud rode down a sky pregnant with storm. And, with every footstep, there grew within me a clarity, wild and new:

This is not my place. I am in the wrong movie. I do not want to be here, do not want to decipher the alphabet of the bloody history that Ferdinand dreams aloud in his alcoholic dreams: Imix—Akbal—Chicchan —Ix—Ben—Ahan—Chuen—Canac.

It is his alone. I have only been a passenger.

I clung tightly to the wall and peered down to see where the laughing voices were coming from, Oliver among them. I could see the children disappear and reemerge between the thousand pillars of the Acropolis. They were playing catch, and with their loud shrieking and laughter they filled out the strange, sultry expectation I was sensing. Freed completely from the phantom of the warrior legacy, they set themselves down in the maw of the Plumed Serpent, hid themselves behind the jaguar enthroned above it, jumped contentedly and cluelessly across the bed of blood trenches.

I climbed further, all the way up; in front of the portal of the Castillo of Queztzlcoatl-Kukulcán, the sacred stone object was sitting in majesty, the bloody symbol of power. And right next to it stood Ferdinand, crowned by a leaden sky. He stood there firmly, grinning, in front of his palace, in his limbs the strained certainty of a mescal high, danced about by peyote smoke from his pipe.

Where had he come from? As if he had flown in. There were four symmetrical stairways leading up, yet I had not seen him coming.

You're amazed, aren't you? he called over to me, as if answering my thoughts.

You have to picture it all in an unbelievable profusion of color. Every stone consecrated to some divinity, every gargoyle animal or human, messenger of life or of death.

He laughed, Mephisto laughed, enticed me up toward him. The moment I got there, he pressed me firmly to himself. From the forest below, voices shot up to us. The shrieking of all sorts of beasts mingled with the cries of the children.

He absolutely had to show me something fantastic, Ferdinand said, and pushed me out in front of him. We stooped our way into the cold room. I was curious, and at the same time horrified.

A few steps. In the interior I came to a frightened halt. In the steel-blue twilight crouched a stone Chac Mool. The stare of his dark pupils drilled through me, an impudent grin on his face. Ferdinand grinned, too, left me no time, pulled me along, further, deeper into the next room, the Cella. Light pressed its way in from somewhere, laid itself like a carpet across to the middle of the stone floor. And there, all by itself, stood the Jaguar Throne, blood-red, ornamented with sheets of milky green jade. From its open maw snarled white bone teeth. A lizard whisked across my foot. I gave a startled cry, but Ferdinand laughingly shoved me toward the throne in the center.

My eyes grew accustomed to the green twilight in the stone chamber. It smelled moist, musty. No sound penetrated the walls. Ferdinand spread his jacket out on the red throne. I lay down upon it. I had made a decision that gave me my fate back. I was no victim.

I drew Ferdinand's body down upon me; with his weight, I could feel how lust warmed my new feelings, and at the same time I felt revenge. Lust, and lust for revenge. I opened my sex as a parting gift. I was the goddess of longing and of the impossible, freedom my gown. Startled bats raced about our wedding of Eros and Despair.

Twelfth century, Toltec, said Ferdinand with a grin as he stood back up, and pointed to the throne. I am the only man who has ever screwed his wife on the Seat of the Gods.

He buttoned up his trousers and extended me his hand to pull me up from the love throne. He kissed me on the mouth, clicked his tongue, and went whistling through one room after another, into the outdoors.

Outside, on the platform, his back to me, he came to a stop. His silhouette against the sky gray. As he pulled on his jacket it seemed for a moment as if he had wings and the air were carrying him off, up, up and away.

He fumbled in his pockets, lay his head back, and took a long gulp from his flask. Which potion, which altered state? Kopal—coca leaves. Peyote. White powder. Mescal. The scent of accursed incense... I saw him still standing there.

As I stepped out through the portal, Ferdinand had disappeared. It was inevitable; I would have been shocked if it had gone any other way. He vanished as quickly as if it had all been a mirage. Only a little cloud of smoke, deep below me, showed that he had just gone around the corner.

From my high perch I stared across at the ball field. Flames threw orange-red light. Princes and dignitaries sat there in the intoxication of their magnificent vestments, between the gaping maws of the Plumed Serpents. Smoke pillars of copal sap spiraled in the air. Naked brown figures, clad only in a cloth, armed with sticks, batted a ball about. Priests with colorfully painted masks of human skulls beat drums of wood, gusted sharply into trumpets, played on bone flutes, blew into horns made of sea snails. Sugar corpses sprang about in a mad dance; women on stilts, little bells on their legs, whirled in a circle. Madonna, with her garland of roses, laughed in the mask of the moon goddess Ixchel. Obsidian knife cut the heart out of Gonzales. The little foot beneath the blue skirt; a rabbit's silent toothy grin; the white water-carrier. The bloody trace of the birth, the shrill scream.

A shrill scream flew up to me, and, with the distinctness of an oracle, I could see Ferdinand down below, clothed only in a loincloth. An exile among the victims, who took up no space, their language not spoken. A small part of the ceremonial mosaic.

He danced about the Serpent Prince, Ah Kin Mai; his breast was bloody; his feet hovered above the red sand, carried aloft by mescal.

Next to me sat a raven and whispered in my ear. Look down there, Phoenix after the devastating fall, in his brilliant self-presentation.

Hernando Cortés's white horse, Morzillo, raced past, hurriedly carrying the God of Thunder and Lightning off with him. And, although I could not account for it, it was a vindication.

Far below me, cloud shadows chased grass scars across sand tables. The smoke of Ferdinand's pipe pointed a long finger at Oliver, who, followed by a horde of Indian children, clung firmly to an imaginary steering wheel, went in faster and faster circles. An explosion of love drowned every feeling of loss within me. The image pulsated before my eyes. The voices of the children, Oliver's laughter, his dear face, a mirror image of Ferdinand's—it all leaped up to me, like music.

He'll grow up to be a race-car driver, I thought, and had to smile. And I felt myself liberated, as if I had finally returned from a long journey. I could see it before me: my wondrous tomorrow, perfect in movement and form. Without any effort on my part, it rolled onward, laid itself at my feet and called out: come along.

The rain suddenly broke loose, a white sheet.

What I Still Wanted to Say

THERE IS A PROBLEM ONE MUST OVERCOME: conceding to the life one has led an importance worth narration. One must believe very strongly in one's own story. Since it lies behind one, since one has dealt with it, it appears now to have been devoured by banality. Thus one can do past events an injustice, even though they were the formative ones, falsely consider them a ladder that one can move to the side, because one forgets that it was on precisely this ladder that one started up life's true path.

Remembrance can be something very corporeal. When I see my sons Oliver and Daniel, who are now grown men, they would tell me something about Ferdinand, should I wish to see it that way.

Was Ferdinand like my father? Perhaps not in his character, but still in gestures that brought him so near to me? Affinity of attraction?

Ferdinand was grandiose, fragile at the same time. He always wanted to please. For that he would have stolen. Fritz on the other hand cared little what others thought of him. What mattered to him was acting justly.

Was it the weaknesses that hid beneath a male pelt, that showed themselves so differently that they fit only into the philosophy of remembrance? My father never revealed his feelings. It was a kind of false manliness, stretching back to his upbringing. And he could not easily give himself over to the natural love my mother bore within herself, like a gift.

Ferdinand, on the other hand, not wanting to come to grips with the wilderness of his emotions, fled into drugs and alcohol. They were not alike, and yet both summoned up within me the feeling of powerlessness and also the wish to rescue—perhaps. Did Ferdinand drown his sorrows because they would otherwise have drowned him? Was Fritz overly punctilious because he, too, was in danger of succumbing? Neither could escape, each for his own reason.

•

When we arrived back from the long journey through Mexico, hauled our suitcases up the stairs, we both looked at the clock.

I have to get going right away, I called out. I have to see Daniel.

I drove two hours, to my brother's house. It must have been dark when I arrived, for his children—he had five sons—were already, or still, asleep. My Daniel, the youngest of them all, lay in a crib. I bent over him, and now, at this moment, I can evoke the feeling of pure happiness that ran through me. I laid my hand on his little chest, to feel his breath. Whereupon he opened his eyes and said: Mami.

It was two more years before Ferdinand and I finally parted ways. I was playing the lead in a film: *Until the Happy End*, a drama about a family secret. The director's name was Theo Kotulla. It was the era of *die Jungfilmer*, the "new German cinema" avant-garde, 1968 or so: Fassbinder, Schlöndorff, Herzog, film festivals in Oberhausen. Fassbinder wanted to induct me into his intellectual "harem," but between one alcoholic and another I was far too traumatized.

I received what for those days was a substantial check. This money made me strong and free. Ferdinand felt threatened by this independence.

When I came home from the film set, late one night, the children ran sobbing toward me:

Papi said you are not coming home to us any more, you are a film star now.

Ferdinand was ensconced in the living room, liquor bottle before him on the table. He was preoccupied with cleaning his pipe.

Ah, there you are, Film Star. His gaze ran dully across the table. Pipes, *idoles*, liquor bottles, me.

The place is suffocating, I said, and went to the window.

This scene is a rerun, I thought. It reminds me of the visit by the American, when Ferdinand robbed me of my autonomy as an artist. *Who gives a shit who the painter is around here...*

Ferdinand there at the table. The empty gaze, so hopeless. And I could very clearly recognize his disease: the addiction that seeks ever further and never finds satisfaction, not even through love.

I took Oliver by the hand, Daniel on my arm, and went out through the door.

I think it was during this night that he signed a letter allowing me to leave him and take the children with me. This was how the law wished it in those days.

•

Years later, after Fritz's death, the period of my mother's great travels began. North America, South America, and, above all, his beloved Africa. There, she visited my sister, Anita, many times, and became an expert, like Fritz before her.

My mother wove into Fritz's Africa stories her own romance of light and shadow in the coffee undergrowth. Yellow adders hidden in borrowed yellow. Millions of helicopter-like seeds straying into one's hair. The enigmatic sigh of the garden after the rains, broken by the shrill applause of an ape family in the mango tree. The murderous paws of a cheetah, in spotted gloves, hanging amid the flight of branches—motionless. And, a little higher up, amid the green and black, his cruel, bored eye.

Ah, and the heat, which she had longed for in cold Bavaria, and which she found superb. That, too, she shared with Fritz.

Always, all her life, she had clung tightly to her humor and encouraged Fritz with it. Like a good tennis match: even when the ball came from the wrong angle, she caught it, or stepped aside. For that reason, too, and yet in such different ways, they were made for one another, right up to the end.

I tell you, my mother could tame ravens. She played with her optimism, and I can still hear the enthusiastic applause for the afternoon apple cake that she rashly served up for guests on the table outside, in the garden, even though it was already thundering—whereupon a pummeling rain filled the forgotten sugar bowl to overflowing.

•

I only saw Ferdinand one more time, thirty years later, in a theatre in Munich, when we celebrated the premier of Daniel's film "Hearts Lonely Hunters." I felt a gaze burning into my back, and, when I turned around, I caught his eye in the darkness behind us. When the audience's faces were no longer illuminated by the screen, as the film ended and the lights came up, I turned around once again. He had vanished.

> Still without forgiveness like Ek Chuah with his spear,
> Vain like Yum Kaax, with the headdress of quezal feathers,
> Like Kinich Ahau with the jaguar, blind in one eye,
> Like Mayahuel, Goddess of Drunkards,
> You had disappeared, soundlessly, like a magician. Genius? Thief?

•

Only in the future has one not yet lost anything. And, one imagines, there will be no repetitions of old mistakes after we have so thoroughly worked through so many experiences and learned from them.

At least you hope so. Then you look back from the present, and say: Let me not neglect this conquest.

A Thank-You Note

MANY PEOPLE WHO READ *A Piece of Me* encouraged me to tell more of the story. I hesitated at first—living life is so self-evident that one forgets the dramas that make up the whole. I must thank many special people who helped me with the great challenge:

Many thanks to Lianne Kolf, who, after the appearance of my childhood memoir, *A Piece of Me*, challenged me: Think about the years that followed; there you will surely find plenty.

To Ruth Greenstein, without whose expert help I would have been stifled by the sheer weight of memory.

To Tenzin Bob Thurman, the closest I will ever come to a guru.

To my dear friend Andrew Solomon, master scribe of the human soul.

To Sigrid Rothe and Sonja Gilkey Weber, my patient German-speaking listeners.

To Sanda Weigl, who tilled through the manuscript with red ink.

To Vera Graaf—"Don't forget yourself."

To Keto von Waberer—"Go where it hurts."

To Sheila Metzner—who can isolate the beauty hidden in devastation

To Gabriel Halevy, with his critical aesthetic eye and knowledge of human nature.

To Camilla Carr, master storyteller on both screen and page.

To Barbara Epler of New Directions, my brilliant, darling friend with the tantalizing mind born for literature.

To Jan Karon—whom I admire very much.

To my wonderful friend Jonathan McVity, who translated the manuscript into English.